# The
# Colorado
# 14ers
## The Standard Routes

Waterfall on South Colony Creek below Crestone Needle, sunset.

THE COLORADO
MOUNTAIN CLUB
GUIDEBOOK

# The Colorado 14ers

## The Standard Routes

# THE COLORADO
# MOUNTAIN CLUB FOUNDATION

The Colorado Mountain Club Press
Golden, Colorado

*The Colorado 14ers: The Standard Routes*

PUBLISHED BY

The Colorado Mountain Club Press
710 Tenth Street, #200, Golden, Colorado 80401
303-996-2743; 1-800-633-4417 | email: cmcpress@cmc.org | www.cmc.org

Founded in 1912, The Colorado Mountain Club is the largest outdoor recreation, education, and conservation organization in the Rocky Mountains. Look for our books at your local bookstore or outdoor retailer or online at www.cmc.org

CONTACTING THE PUBLISHER
We would appreciate it if readers would alert us to any errors or outdated information by contacting us at the address above.

| | |
|---|---|
| Alan Bernhard | design, composition, and production |
| Todd Caudle | photographer |
| Michelle Myers | copyeditor |
| Suzanne Najarian | proofreader |
| Alan Stark | publisher |

Cover/title page photo of Crestone Needle by Todd Caudle. www.skylinepress.com

DISTRIBUTED TO THE BOOK TRADE BY

Mountaineers Books
1001 SW Klickitat Way, Suite 201, Seattle, WA 98134, 800-553-4453,
www.mountaineersbooks.org

We gratefully acknowledge the financial support of the people of Colorado through the Scientific and Cultural Facilities District of greater metropolitan Denver for our publishing activities.

TOPOGRAPHIC MAPS are copyright 2010 and were created using National Geographic TOPO! Outdoor Recreation Mapping Software. 800-962-1643, www.natgeomaps.com

The primary source of the routes depicted on the maps in this book was 14ers.com (www.14ers.com) and the Colorado Fourteeners Initiative (www.14ers.org).

Historical notes adapted from *A Climbing Guide to Colorado's Fourteeners* by Walter R. Borneman and Lyndon J. Lampert.

ISBN 978-0-9799663-8-5

Printed in Korea

# Contents

LOCATOR MAP . . . . . . . . . . . . . . . . . . . . . . . . . . . . . . . . . . . . . . . . 8–9

AN INTRODUCTION TO THE FOURTEENERS . . . . . . . . . . . . . . . . . . . 10

## FRONT RANGE

Longs Peak. . . . . . . . . . . . . . . . . . . . . . . . . . . . . . . . . . . . . . . . . . . . . . . 22
Grays Peak . . . . . . . . . . . . . . . . . . . . . . . . . . . . . . . . . . . . . . . . . . . . . . . 26
Torreys Peak . . . . . . . . . . . . . . . . . . . . . . . . . . . . . . . . . . . . . . . . . . . . . 26
Mount Evans. . . . . . . . . . . . . . . . . . . . . . . . . . . . . . . . . . . . . . . . . . . . . 30
Mount Bierstadt. . . . . . . . . . . . . . . . . . . . . . . . . . . . . . . . . . . . . . . . . . 34
Pikes Peak. . . . . . . . . . . . . . . . . . . . . . . . . . . . . . . . . . . . . . . . . . . . . . . 38

## SANGRE DE CRISTO RANGE

Kit Carson Peak . . . . . . . . . . . . . . . . . . . . . . . . . . . . . . . . . . . . . . . . . . 42
Humboldt Peak. . . . . . . . . . . . . . . . . . . . . . . . . . . . . . . . . . . . . . . . . . . 46
Crestone Peak . . . . . . . . . . . . . . . . . . . . . . . . . . . . . . . . . . . . . . . . . . . 50
Crestone Needle . . . . . . . . . . . . . . . . . . . . . . . . . . . . . . . . . . . . . . . . . 54
Mount Lindsey . . . . . . . . . . . . . . . . . . . . . . . . . . . . . . . . . . . . . . . . . . . 58
Little Bear Peak . . . . . . . . . . . . . . . . . . . . . . . . . . . . . . . . . . . . . . . . . . 62
Blanca Peak. . . . . . . . . . . . . . . . . . . . . . . . . . . . . . . . . . . . . . . . . . . . . . 66
Ellingwood Point. . . . . . . . . . . . . . . . . . . . . . . . . . . . . . . . . . . . . . . . . 66
Culebra Peak . . . . . . . . . . . . . . . . . . . . . . . . . . . . . . . . . . . . . . . . . . . . 70

## TENMILE AND MOSQUITO RANGES

Quandary Peak. . . . . . . . . . . . . . . . . . . . . . . . . . . . . . . . . . . . . . . . . . . 74
Mount Democrat. . . . . . . . . . . . . . . . . . . . . . . . . . . . . . . . . . . . . . . . . 78
Mount Lincoln. . . . . . . . . . . . . . . . . . . . . . . . . . . . . . . . . . . . . . . . . . . 78
Mount Bross . . . . . . . . . . . . . . . . . . . . . . . . . . . . . . . . . . . . . . . . . . . . . 78
Mount Sherman. . . . . . . . . . . . . . . . . . . . . . . . . . . . . . . . . . . . . . . . . . 82

## SAWATCH RANGE

Mount of the Holy Cross. . . . . . . . . . . . . . . . . . . . . . . . . . . . . . . . . . . 86
Mount Massive . . . . . . . . . . . . . . . . . . . . . . . . . . . . . . . . . . . . . . . . . . 90

Mount Elbert ............................................................. 94
La Plata Peak ........................................................... 98
Mount Belford ......................................................... 102
Mount Oxford .......................................................... 102
Missouri Mountain ................................................... 106
Huron Peak ............................................................. 110
Mount Harvard ........................................................ 114
Mount Columbia ...................................................... 114
Mount Yale ............................................................. 118
Mount Princeton ...................................................... 122
Mount Antero ......................................................... 126
Mount Shavano ....................................................... 130
Tabeguache Peak ..................................................... 130

## ELK MOUNTAINS

Capitol Peak ........................................................... 134
Snowmass Mountain .................................................. 138
North Maroon Peak ................................................... 142
(South) Maroon Peak ................................................. 146
Pyramid Peak .......................................................... 150
Castle Peak ............................................................ 154

## SAN JUAN MOUNTAINS

San Luis Peak ......................................................... 158
Uncompahgre Peak .................................................... 162
Wetterhorn Peak ...................................................... 166
Redcloud Peak ........................................................ 170
Sunshine Peak ......................................................... 170
Handies Peak .......................................................... 174
Sunlight Peak ......................................................... 178
Windom Peak .......................................................... 178
Mount Eolus .......................................................... 182
Mount Sneffels ........................................................ 186
Wilson Peak ........................................................... 190
Mount Wilson ......................................................... 194
El Diente Peak ........................................................ 198

## SIDEBARS

Interstate 70 .................................................. 29
Ride a Fourteener .............................................. 33
The Dreaded Willows ........................................... 36
12,000 Foot Mantra ............................................ 44
The Road ...................................................... 48
Really Stupid? ................................................. 64
Cell Phones ................................................... 69
A Day to Acclimate ............................................ 76
Trail Right-of-Way ............................................. 84
Boots ......................................................... 92
When You Are Feeling Pukey .................................... 100
Summit Time ................................................... 108
That Gurgling Sound ........................................... 113
A Lightning Protocol .......................................... 120
Gearing Up in the Dark ........................................ 124
Oh Buddy, We Can Make It ...................................... 136
Polypro ....................................................... 144
The Rest Step ................................................. 164
Water ......................................................... 168


**ANNOTATED BIBLIOGRAPHY** ..................................... 202

**GLOSSARY** .................................................. 204


**APPENDIX 1**
Colorado Fourteeners Ranked by Height ......................... 205


**APPENDIX 2**
Colorado Fourteeners Climbing Tick List ....................... 207

# COLORADO 14ers LOCATOR MAP

## FRONT RANGE
1  Longs Peak
2  Grays Peak
3  Torreys Peak
4  Mount Evans
5  Mount Bierstadt
6  Pikes Peak

## SANGRE DE CRISTO RANGE
7  Kit Carson Peak
8  Humboldt Peak
9  Crestone Peak
10  Crestone Needle
11  Mount Lindsey
12  Little Bear Peak
13  Blanca Peak
14  Ellingwood Point
15  Culebra Peak

## TENMILE AND MOSQUITO RANGES
16  Quandary Peak
17  Mount Democrat
18  Mount Lincoln
19  Mount Bross
20  Mount Sherman

## SAWATCH RANGE
21  Mount of the Holy Cross
22  Mount Massive
23  Mount Elbert
24  La Plata Peak
25  Mount Belford
26  Mount Oxford
27  Missouri Mountain
28  Huron Peak
29  Mount Harvard
30  Mount Columbia
31  Mount Yale
32  Mount Princeton
33  Mount Antero
34  Mount Shavano
35  Tabeguache Peak

## ELK MOUNTAINS
36  Capitol Peak
37  Snowmass Mountain
38  North Maroon Peak
39  (South) Maroon Peak
40  Pyramid Peak
41  Castle Peak

## SAN JUAN MOUNTAINS
42  San Luis Peak
43  Uncompahgre Peak
44  Wetterhorn Peak
45  Redcloud Peak
46  Sunshine Peak
47  Handies Peak
48  Sunlight Peak
49  Windom Peak
50  Mount Eolus
51  Mount Sneffels
52  Wilson Peak
53  Mount Wilson
54  El Diente Peak

Marsh marigolds.

# An Introduction to the Fourteeners

There are several possible reasons for you to have acquired this book: (1) You are thinking about climbing a Colorado Fourteener and are looking for some basic information; (2) You have done some of the Fourteeners and are always interested in a new guidebook; or (3) You are trying to impress people and think it might be cool to have a climbing guide on your coffee table to show everyone what a badass you are.

This third edition of *The Colorado 14ers* is designed for all three.

If you are considering climbing a Fourteener for the first time, we suggest that you select one of the more moderate routes that we have marked, surprisingly enough, as "Moderate." There are all sorts of routes up the Fourteeners, and the routes that are considered "standard" are almost always the easiest routes up the mountain. The more serious among us call them "trade routes," because they get so much traffic, or "dog routes," because most of the Fourteeners can be climbed by a dog (and have been).

These are also the routes recommended by the Colorado Fourteeners Initiative (CFI) and the US Forest Service (USFS) as the most sustainable routes up the mountains that do the least environmental damage. "Wait," you're thinking. "How can a climber cause environmental damage?" In general, it's not about you, because you stay on durable surfaces like rock and snow, you don't walk beside a trail because it's muddy, and you don't shortcut switchbacks because it's faster. It's much more about the carrying capacity of these high-altitude trails and the fact that more than 500,000 people per summer attempt at least one Fourteener. Did we mention that many of these trails are braided and that these multiple trails all headed generally in the same direction tend to erode during spring runoff and summer thunderstorms? And it should be obvious that many of the plants that grow at altitude don't do well when repeatedly stomped.

Additionally, if you are a climber who is new to the Fourteeners, there is some real basic stuff that you should understand before attempting any of the routes, such as acclimatization, hydration, nutrition, and being off the summit by noon. Our various and sundry sidebars talk about this basic information, and we encourage you to read all of them. We also encourage you to get a copy of *Mountaineering: The Freedom of the Hills* from Mountaineers Books and read and understand the first four or five chapters.

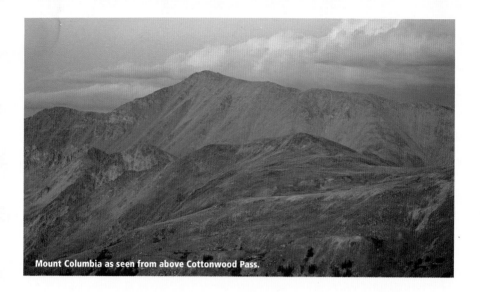

Mount Columbia as seen from above Cottonwood Pass.

If you are a climber with some Fourteener experience, our guess is that you already have a guidebook or a Fourteener web site that you use for routes. In fact, if you are like us, you have just about every book written on the Fourteeners and this book is just a colorful addition to your collection. We hope you enjoy it and that your significant other doesn't find out that you have purchased yet another guidebook. We know the web is a wonderful tool, but we're throwbacks and think that the best possible tool for thinking and dreaming about mountains is a well-designed guidebook.

But we had another goal in mind. We wanted you to have an easy reference to the mountains that you haven't climbed. We want you to use our book as a primer on Fourteeners, and once you have selected a mountain, we want to expose you to the standard route and encourage you to take it. But we also understand that you may be looking for more of a challenge or more details than are possible under the rubric of a primer. As you probably know, for more detail you can't beat Gerry Roach's *Colorado's Fourteeners* that is due out in a third edition, and for the ultimate in detail, go to Bill Middlebrook's 14ers.com. And if you are a skier, beg, borrow, or steal *Dawson's Guide to Colorado's Fourteeners* by Louis W. Dawson II. Both volumes are out of print, but are available in libraries and on the web.

And while we don't think there is any real hope for those of you who want to impress companions with guidebooks on your coffee table, we wanted our book to look good against the competition. To this end, we have come up with some really fine pictures by Todd Caudle, who has spent most of his career photographing Colorado, and have included colorful route maps that we developed using TOPO! Outdoor Recreation Mapping Software from the fine folks at National Geographic Maps, who also publish Trails Illustrated maps. And we wish you luck at being a badass.

We asked climber and noted historian Walt Borneman to write some overall historical notes, which follow, and to also attempt to explain how each of the Fourteeners may have been named. Walt, along with Lyndon Lampert, wrote the most successful Fourteener guide of the '70s and '80s: *A Climbing Guide to Colorado's Fourteeners.*

## HISTORY

The Fourteeners stretch across Colorado from Longs Peak in the Front Range, in sight of Wyoming; to Culebra Peak, just north of New Mexico; to the San Juan Range near the famous Four Corners area, where Colorado, Arizona, New Mexico, and Utah meet. Climbing the Fourteeners will take you to many parts of Colorado and will introduce you to a variety of flora, fauna, and rock, and even a little history.

An arrowhead found on the boulder field below the summit of Longs Peak and a man-made shelter discovered at the apex of Blanca yield evidence that Native Americans did climb Colorado's great mountains.

Members of several surveys, especially the Hayden and Wheeler surveys, climbed many of the Fourteeners. A survey team climbed and named Mount Harvard and Mount Yale in 1869, while Mount Massive and Mount Elbert were summited in 1874.

Trappers and miners also climbed some of the great mountains, and prospect holes were found near the summits of Handies Peak and Mount Bierstadt, while abandoned cabins and mines dot the flanks of Mount Democrat and Mount Lincoln. Early climbers discovered evidence that grizzly bears may have used the summits of several peaks as habitat. A she-grizzly "came rushing past us," reported a climber nearing the summit of Uncompahgre Peak in 1874, and claw marks were discovered on the rock near the summit of Mount Sneffels.

The first record of someone climbing all of the then-known Fourteeners in Colorado dates to 1923, when Carl Blaurock and William Ervin achieved this feat. In 1912, Blaurock was one of the charter members of The Colorado Mountain Club (CMC), whose history is intimately tied to the exploration, mapping, and even naming of Colorado's mountains.

How many Fourteeners are there? That is a question that has intrigued climbers since the early days of exploration. A guide published in 1925 lists 47. Included in this ranking are Stewart Peak in the San Juan Range and Grizzly Peak in the Sawatch Range, which later were demoted to Thirteeners. Missouri Mountain and its neighbor, Huron Peak, were added to the list in the mid-1950s after new measurements were made by the United States Geological Survey (USGS). Mount of the Holy Cross appeared on the list, was taken off, and then reinstated. By 1972, 53 peaks were recognized as Fourteeners. Ellingwood Point in the Sangre de Cristo Range was the last peak to be added to the list. Today, 54 mountains are recognized as Fourteeners, both by the USGS and by the CMC.

## HOW TO USE THIS GUIDEBOOK

The organization of this book is straightforward. The peaks are grouped by the ranges in which they are found, and the ranges are listed from east to west across Colorado. Within each range the peaks are cited from north to south.

The information on **MAPS** at the top of each description includes the USGS 7.5 minute map(s) as well as the Trails Illustrated map that you will need to do the route. The maps in this book are approximations that are only meant to give a general direction of the route. (See the **WARNING** on the copyright page.) Note that the trails in this book often follow the routes marked on the USGS quads, but sometimes they don't follow the USGS routes because the trail has been moved since the map was produced. After this book is published, some of these trails will be rerouted to lessen environmental impact. Check with the Colorado Fourteeners Initiative for up-to-date information about route changes. Always have USGS quad maps or a Trails Illustrated map of the mountain you are climbing. Using this and other guidebooks and web sites, sketch the route. And remember that route-finding is part of the adventure, and that if the route gets real difficult quickly, you are probably off-route, lost, and need to back up. Maps are available through your local outdoor store, or from www.usgs.gov for 7.5 minute quad maps and www.natgeomaps.com for Trails Illustrated maps.

The climbers who have shared their knowledge of the Colorado

Fourteeners and suggested **RATINGS** in this book maintain that there really are no "easy" mountains. Slippery cliffs, falling rock, crumbling ledges, heaving talus slopes, and abrupt changes in the weather can turn a pleasant hike into a difficult climb. Thus, none of the mountains is rated as "easy" to climb. Our ratings are "Moderate," "More difficult," and "Very difficult," all relative terms depending on weather, the climber's physical condition, and the time of the year. We do make a point, however, of telling you if a mountain is more difficult and if the climb can be particularly dangerous.

**ELEVATION GAINS** are self-explanatory. Where two peaks are traditionally climbed in one day, the elevation gain and **ROUND-TRIP DISTANCE** are recorded for doing both mountains. The elevation gains depend on where you start or where you camp; the ones listed here are estimates. Note that on some of these routes there is a substantial loss of altitude on the approach.

The estimated **ROUND-TRIP DISTANCE** and estimated **ROUND-TRIP TIME** are just that: estimates. The **NEAREST TOWN** is a recognizable town on a Colorado state road map. We've also included the **RANGER DISTRICT** in which each route is located, or contact information if the land is privately owned.

Descriptions start out with a **COMMENT**. These comments typically note mountains that are done together, difficult routes that require traditional climbing gear, objective dangers, mountains with roads to the top, and the name of the standard route.

**GETTING THERE** is a section that describes how to get to the trailhead and, often, where to park once you are there. Some of these routes require four-wheel-drive vehicles with good clearance. We are not kidding about four-wheel-drive roads. The locals are vastly entertained when they come upon a rental subcompact on its side. And if you rent a four-wheel-drive at Denver International Airport, be careful; driving these roads is a little more tricky than you might imagine, particularly when they are wet.

The **ROUTES** described here are for summer and early autumn trips. Winter conditions can alter not only the route but also the entire climbing experience. Distances are round-trip distances except when noted otherwise.

The **HISTORY** section contains notes on the naming of the mountain provided by Walt Borneman, and **SIDEBARS** consist of occasional observations, thoughts, or rants that you might find useful when climbing the Fourteeners.

# CLIMBING THE FOURTEENERS

When you consider climbing a Fourteener, the words challenge, fun, and adventure all come to mind. Indeed, those of us involved in producing this book have felt and enjoyed all of that and more in the High Country. But we also ask you to be serious about climbing Fourteeners and keep in mind such words as danger, disaster, and pain. If you are sick, hurt, or disabled on a Fourteener, getting down can be problematic. Our friends in mountain rescue groups, county sheriff's departments, and federal agencies have risked a great deal over the years to bring broken or lifeless bodies down from the Fourteeners. Don't let that be you. Here are some of the truths about climbing Fourteeners that should concern you:

Route descriptions cannot be relied upon as a substitute for good judgment and careful preparation. The guidebook makes no provision for the many variables that affect a climb, such as weather, the physical condition of the participants, and the possibility that climbers will fail to locate the described landmarks.

You should use this guide with discretion and awareness of the countless hazards and challenges that must be confronted on even the "easiest" climbs. High mountains are subject to abrupt and drastic weather changes. Afternoon lightning storms should always be expected when climbing the Fourteeners from April to September, and some peaks do seem to have more storms than others. These peaks are identified in the text.

Due to the frequency of early afternoon storms, summer climbs should be planned so that the party is descending from the summit by noon.

Despite what anyone may tell you, breathing almost three miles above sea level or climbing several miles upward at a high altitude will not only take your breath away, it will tire you quickly. The more serious physical discomforts high-altitude climbers may encounter are nausea, headache, and, occasionally, heart palpitations and dis-orientation. There is an inherent risk in climbing mountains. Each climber attempting a Fourteener should be aware of the risk.

High altitude almost always means low temperatures and strong winds. Therefore, frostbite and hypothermia are possible dangers. You can become exhausted or lost, or you may find yourself facing cliffs that require technical rock-climbing skills. The consequences of climbing beyond your ability can be severe; if you do so you not only expose yourself to injury but also endanger those hiking with you or coming to your assistance if you cannot go on.

We climb to challenge the limits of our bodies and our wills, and to test our capacity for risks. Yet, to go unprepared—to carry no maps or compass, to take an inadequate amount of water, or to eschew a pack with warm clothing and rain gear—is simply dumb. On a Fourteener, a cloudless, sunny day can rapidly change to a snowstorm or a whiteout, drinking unpurified stream water can expose you to waterborne parasites, and a lightning strike can ruin your day.

Be careful up there.

## ACCESS TO THE FOURTEENERS

As of the editing of this book in Fall 2009, there is no access to the summit of Mount Bross. Access to Culebra Peak is limited and on a fee basis. Check with the Colorado Fourteeners Initiative (14ers.org) for up-to-date information.

On a number of Fourteener routes, you will be passing near or over private property. This access, if abused in any way, can and has been denied over the years. You are an adult and you are responsible. Tread lightly on private property and treat it and the owners with respect.

## THE 10 ESSENTIALS

A properly equipped hiker will more likely than not have a successful outing. Essential equipment includes: broken-in hiking boots over wool socks on your feet and an extra pair of socks, wool or polypro, in your pack; quick-drying pants or rain pants, not cotton jeans; a lightweight wool or polypro shirt, not cotton; a hooded waterproof jacket or parka; a warm head covering and gloves; and plenty of water, plus at least one meal and additional snacks.

The CMC adopted a list years ago, compiled by the Mountaineers of Seattle, of the "10 Essentials" that hikers and mountain climbers should carry in their day-packs or backpacks.

| These essentials are: | A more modern list goes this way: |
|---|---|
| 1. Map | 1. Navigation |
| 2. Compass | 2. Illumination |
| 3. Flashlight or headlamp | 3. Hydration |

4. Extra food
5. Sun protection—hat, sunglasses, sunscreen
6. Extra clothing
7. Small first aid kit
8. Pocket knife
9. Matches
10. Fire starter

4. Nutrition
5. Sun protection
6. Insulation
7. First aid
8. Repair kit
9. Fire
10. Shelter

There are other lists, but you get the point. You need this stuff to survive the worst that the Fourteeners can hand out. If you think you cannot carry the extra weight, perhaps you should reconsider your decision to climb a Fourteener in the first place. Some of the peaks require the use of a helmet, a rope, and occasionally, an ice axe. Climbers attempting these mountains should be familiar with belay and self-arrest techniques. It is also imperative that you tell a family member or friend where you are going and when you expect to return. And don't forget to sign in at the trailhead if a register is available.

## THE COLORADO MOUNTAIN CLUB

The CMC began placing registers on the peaks of the Fourteeners in the 1910s and 1920s. Old registers, which are available to researchers, are archived at the American Mountaineering Center in Golden, Colorado. Registers from the early years of the twentieth century show that the number of climbers scaling the Fourteeners remained fairly constant until the 1950s. Climbing increased in popularity in the 1960s and 1970s, and exploded in the 1980s and 1990s. On a popular mountain such as Longs Peak, a register with room for 500 names fills in a week.

Registers are rolled up and stored in PVC plastic canisters secured at the summit by a cable or rock. Sometimes it is difficult to find the small, inconspicuous gray tube. Once you locate the canister, sign your name with a ballpoint pen or with a pencil. Signatures made with other sorts of pens tend to bleed on the entire register and obliterate names.

CMC members and CMC Press have also produced a number of mountain guides to Colorado's Rockies. The most exhaustive guide is the tenth edition of the *Guide to the Colorado Mountains,* available at www.cmc.org/store. Several detailed and useful guides to the Fourteeners, compiled by intrepid mountaineers in and outside the CMC, can be ordered by your local bookstore.

John L. Jerome Hart wrote the first history of the naming and early ascents of the Fourteeners in 1925. As climbing Fourteeners grew in popularity, Hart's guide, *Fourteen Thousand Feet*, was reprinted in 1931 and updated in 1972. A new guide, based on Hart's but containing specific routes, was prepared in 1967 by Ray Phillips, another active CMC member. This guide was revised in 1978 by Sally Richards as the editor, with Jim Gehres and Al Ossinger preparing many of the updates. Jim and Al, as well as Giles Toll, are responsible for the trail updates in the previous edition. The crew at the Colorado Fourteeners Initiative, and in particular Greg Seabloom, was helpful in trail updates of this book, and a portion of the royalties from this book will benefit the CFI. This book would not exist without all of their input.

## THE COLORADO MOUNTAIN CLUB FOUNDATION

The Colorado Mountain Club Foundation (CMCF) was created in 1973 and supports expeditions to such far-flung places as the Himalayas and China. Since 1981, the CMCF has given grants to students in college and graduate school doing research in history, geology, geography, biology, and other aspects of Colorado's mountains. The CMCF also provides loans to the Wilderness Land Trust to permit the purchase of land when it becomes available in areas where trail access is restricted. The CMCF publishes brochures to educate hikers on hypothermia, lightning, and snow avalanches, and distributes these materials free of charge to hikers through the CMC, the Forest Service, the National Park Service, and outdoor retailers.

The CMCF also maintains a list of those who have climbed all of the Fourteeners and registered their accomplishment. At the time of publication in the spring of 2010, the list contained 1,320 names.

Individuals active in the CMCF volunteer their time. Contributions to the CMCF are tax deductible. Royalties from this guidebook will benefit the work of the CMCF.

Climbers interested in the work of the CMC or CMCF may obtain further information by contacting the club and the foundation at the American Mountaineering Center, 710 10th Street, Suite 200, Golden, Colorado 80401.

Climbers who have completed all 54 Fourteeners should notify the Colorado Mountain Club Foundation at the above address to register their accomplishment and be included in the annual listing. Remember, an unwritten rule of the CMC is that a valid climb of a Fourteener entails an elevation gain of at least 3,000 feet. As with many rules, there are exceptions, and the 3,000-foot-gain per peak rule does not apply when you are climbing two adjacent mountains, or where the access trail begins at a higher elevation, such as for Mount Bierstadt.

## COLORADO FOURTEENERS INITIATIVE

Since its founding in 1994, the Colorado Fourteeners Initiative has become the nation's leading organization building sustainable trails at high altitudes, restoring damaged tundra, and providing on-mountain education to Fourteener climbers. CFI's projects do not make the Fourteeners any easier to climb, but they protect these unique natural resources from harm to ensure the long-term sustainability of recreation on these peaks.

Colorado's 54 Fourteeners are a magnet for climbers worldwide due to their rugged beauty, varied terrain, and relative ease of access. An estimated 500,000 climbers attempt their summits annually, a number that grows each year. Increased use combined with poorly located trails has resulted in growing environmental impacts on the fragile alpine tundra on these high peaks. Repeated trampling by Fourteener climbers kills native plants and animal habitat—including some plants and animals that exist nowhere else in the world—threatening ecosystems that took millennia to develop.

You can help in the ongoing stewardship of the Fourteeners by following these Leave No Trace practices developed by CFI.

## "LEAVE NO TRACE" HIKING

The Fourteeners are a harsh, yet fragile, environment. Above timberline, plants grow very slowly due to the harsh conditions and short growing seasons. Even slight disturbances can cause long-term damage. Impacted areas may take hundreds—if not thousands—of years to recover.

To minimize environmental impact, hikers should remain on the trail—especially in areas where trail modifications have been made to reduce human impacts. Because of the increased popularity of climbing the Fourteeners, ascents on weekdays not only minimize human impacts but also offer solitude and diminish trail and campground congestion.

The Colorado Fourteeners Initiative has developed these Leave No Trace guidelines that are specific to hiking and climbing the Fourteeners.

### When hiking on a trail:

Stay on existing routes and never cut across switchbacks.

Walk through muddy or snow-covered segments of the trail, not around them.

When encountering braided or parallel trails, use the most impacted or eroded trail.

### When a trail does not exist:

Travel on durable surfaces such as rock, snow and ridges, and avoid gullies or steep and loose slopes, because these are prone to erosion and alpine vegetation loss.

Disperse over a wide area if traveling in a group to minimize the impact of stepping on fragile tundra.

### When camping in alpine basins:

Use existing campsites.

Do not camp above timberline.

Consult CFI's web site—www.14ers.org—for information on recommended routes and updated trail changes, as well as opportunities to become involved in the long-term stewardship of the Fourteeners.

## FINAL NOTE

In this introduction and throughout the guidebook we have talked, and will continue to talk, about safety until you are tired of reading it and begin to think that maybe we are taking ourselves a little too seriously —after all, most of these routes are basically walk-ups. Talk to any mountain rescue type and she or he can tell you 100 different ways to get killed in the mountains, but over the years the big killer has been a slip or fall on rock, snow. or ice. Check out the statistics in the back of any edition of *Accidents in North American Mountaineering* from the American Alpine Club. We have one more thought about climbing, or, for that matter, any endeavor that takes you in harm's way: You often get hurt or killed not by one big thing, but by a lot of little things that go wrong. Think about it.

You wake up with a headache. Two miles out of base camp you remember that you left your rain jacket in the tent. You get off-route and find yourself in a butt-ugly couloir filled with loose rock, and then it starts to cloud over early. You are looking at a lot of mistakes in a row, some of them your fault. What makes you think you'll stop making mistakes? Turn around, carefully retrace your steps, and get off the mountain. It's not your day. The mountain will be there forever. Live to try again tomorrow.

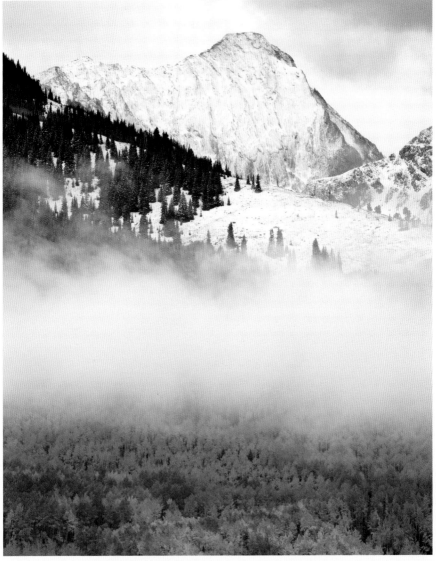

Capitol Peak in autumn from the Capitol Creek Trailhead.

Longs Peak from Rock Cut, along Trail Ridge Road in Rocky Mountain National Park.

# Longs Peak
## 14,255 feet

| MAPS | Trails Illustrated 301–Longs Peak; Longs Peak 7.5 minute |
|---|---|
| RATING | Very difficult |
| ELEVATION GAIN | 4,850 feet |
| ROUND-TRIP DISTANCE | 16 miles |
| ROUND-TRIP TIME | 12 to 15 hours |
| NEAREST TOWN | Estes Park |
| HEADQUARTERS | National Park Service, Rocky Mountain National Park, 970-586-1206 or nps.gov/romo |

**COMMENT:** Plan on a very early start and a very long day. This is the only Colorado Fourteener in a national park. Remember that national park rules apply. The standard route is called the Keyhole Route. The route is rated Very Difficult because most climbers complete the route in one long day.

**GETTING THERE:** Drive south from Estes Park 10 miles on Colorado 7, then 1 mile west to a "T" junction. The left fork leads to the Longs Peak Ranger Station and parking lot, which is often crowded. The right fork leads to the Longs Peak Campground, where sites are available on a first-come basis. Additional camping is available at backcountry sites, where permits are required. Contact the Backcountry Office (970-586-1242) for information.

**THE ROUTE:** The trailhead for Longs is next to the ranger station. Follow a good, moderately steep trail 6 miles west to the Boulder Field at about 12,800 feet. Continue southwest for about 1 mile to the keyhole ridge at 13,100 feet. From here, the route is well marked with yellow and red bull's-eyes (otherwise known as fried eggs). Follow the route onto the ledges along the west side of the peak, up the rock trough to the ledge junction, or spur. Turn southeast through the "narrows" to the "homestretch" of slab rock. Then continue to the large, flat summit. This is a long, tedious climb. There is exposure on the ledges, and the upper mountain can be dangerously slick with ice. Before starting, check with the ranger regarding conditions. At certain times, an ice axe may be needed.

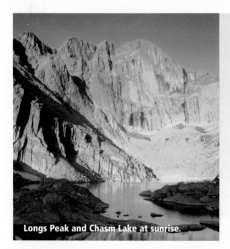

Longs Peak and Chasm Lake at sunrise.

**HISTORY:** In 1820, Major Stephen H. Long led an expedition along Colorado's Front Range, and his name soon became associated with this prominent landmark. On August 23, 1868, a party led by John Wesley Powell finally reached the summit, although Arapaho who were trapping eagles may have preceded this first documented ascent.

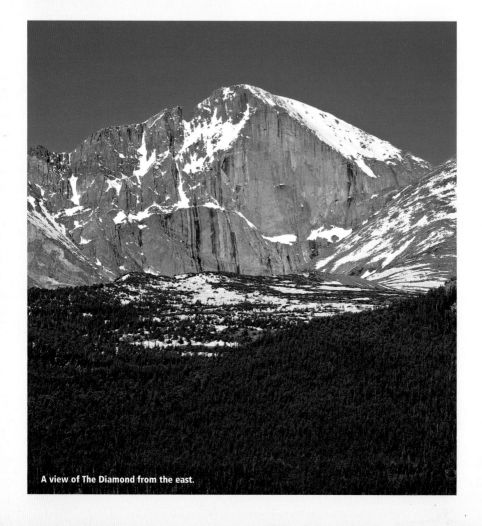

A view of The Diamond from the east.

Grays Peak (left) and Torreys Peak (right) from the northeast, viewed from McClellan Mountain.

# Grays Peak 14,270 feet
# Torreys Peak 14,267 feet

| MAPS | Trails Illustrated 104–Idaho Springs/Georgetown/Loveland Pass; Grays Peak 7.5 minute |
|---|---|
| RATING | Moderate |
| ELEVATION GAIN | 3,000 to 3,600 feet |
| ROUND-TRIP DISTANCE | 8 to 9 miles |
| ROUND-TRIP TIME | 6 to 8 hours |
| NEAREST TOWN | Silver Plume |
| RANGER DISTRICT | US Forest Service, Clear Creek Ranger District, 303-567-3000 |

**COMMENT:** These two peaks can be climbed in one day with little more effort than it takes to climb only one. Weather, of course, can be a factor in deciding whether to attempt both peaks. Stevens Gulch is the standard route. Grays, the peak to the south (left), is usually climbed first. After summiting Grays, you then proceed to the saddle between Grays and Torreys, and climb Torreys. Climbers starting early can drive from Denver and return to the city that same evening.

CFI completed trail construction and restoration work in 2000–2002. Due to heavy use of this route, CFI partners with several Adopt-a-Peak volunteer groups on Grays and Torreys Peaks each year that you may encounter doing trail maintenance. Due to high use, this trail tends to get very wide and braided. Always stay on the main trail, do not cut switchbacks, and if you encounter very wide and/or braided sections of trail, hike single-file on the most eroded/impacted part of the trail to prevent further widening.

**GETTING THERE:** From Denver, drive west on Interstate 70 to Bakerville, Exit 221. Turn left over the interstate and drive south 3.5 miles on a steep, but wide and passable, dirt road to the vicinity of Stevens Mine at 11,300 feet. There is a parking lot for about 30 vehicles, and outhouses are adjacent to the parking lot.

**THE ROUTE:** Take the iron bridge across the stream and follow a good trail that switchbacks for 3.5 miles. At about 13,200 feet, there is a trail junction left and up to Grays. The climber has the choice of continuing up another 0.5 mile to the summit of Grays, or taking the trail west to the saddle between Grays and Torreys at 13,700 feet and climbing Torreys' ridge to the summit.

After climbing Grays, descend from the summit northwest 600 feet into the saddle on a marked trail and follow the ridge north for 0.5 mile to the summit of Torreys. The distance between the peaks is about 0.7 mile as the crow flies.

**HISTORY:** Grays Peak and its neighbor, Torreys Peak, are the only Fourteeners to sit squarely atop the Continental Divide. While Native Americans called these peaks "the Ant Hills," Charles C. Parry renamed them in 1861 for widely respected botanists Asa Gray and John Torrey.

There is usually an extensive snowfield at the saddle in the spring and early summer. Cross the saddle by post-holing. Try to remain on the trail to avoid trampling on the fragile vegetation on the edges of the snowfield. Proceed with caution.

From Torreys, return to the saddle, then work back to the trail down the north side of Grays. Early in the season, this route may entail a climb well up Grays' slope to avoid the usual snow cornice.

You may see mountain goats during the climb.

Because of the climb's popularity and to protect the tundra, the CFI has realigned part of the trail on the saddle. It is marked with cairns.

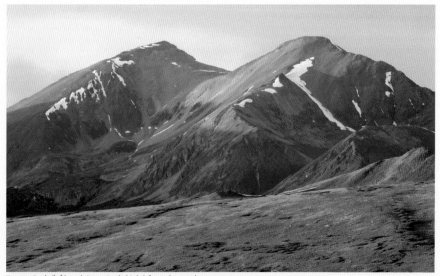

Torreys Peak (left) and Grays Peak (right) from the south at sunset.

## SIDEBAR: INTERSTATE 70

We know. We know. Interstate 5 on the west coast is probably one of the worst roads ever built, and virtually undriveable in a cold winter rainstorm. And I-95 on the east coast, "forget about it," as the locals say. If you can't get out there and play with the 18-wheelers, don't bother.

But we know of nothing quite like I-70 on a Friday or Sunday afternoon. Starting at about 2 p.m. on Friday, I-70 going west slows to a crawl, then becomes a parking lot that doesn't clear up until after dark. The same thing happens in reverse on Sunday afternoon.

To an out-of-town climber, I-70 looks like the best route to the mountains if you land at Denver International Airport. Don't do it if you can avoid it. Check out US 285 out of southwestern Denver and US 24 by way of I-25 south to Colorado Springs. Both are two-lane highways, but tend to move relatively well.

Mount Evans' reflection in Summit Lake

# Mount Evans
## 14,264 feet

| | |
|---|---|
| **MAPS** | Trails Illustrated 104–Idaho Springs/Georgetown/Loveland Pass; Mount Evans 7.5 minute, Idaho Springs 7.5 minute |
| **RATING** | Moderate |
| **ELEVATION GAIN** | 1,400 feet from Summit Lake, 5,000 feet from below Chicago Lakes |
| **ROUND-TRIP DISTANCE** | 5 miles from Summit Lake |
| **ROUND-TRIP TIME** | 4 hours from Summit Lake |
| **NEAREST TOWN** | Georgetown |
| **RANGER DISTRICT** | US Forest Service, Clear Creek Ranger District, 303-567-3000 |

**COMMENT:** Mount Evans has a paved toll road to the top that can be run or cycled, but watch out for the traffic. Since there is a paved road to the summit, there is no register. The standard route starts at Summit Lake and goes over Mount Spalding. The climb can be done in a day trip from Denver.

CFI completed trail construction and restoration work on this route in 2005–2006.

**GETTING THERE:** Take Interstate 70 west to Idaho Springs. Take exit 240 and follow the signs to Mount Evans Road. Park at the Summit Lake Trailhead if there is space available. Get to Chicago Lakes from the Echo Lake Trailhead near the Echo Lake Lodge.

**THE ROUTE:** Start from Summit Lake by hiking northwest around the lake to the start of the established trail up the ridge to Mount Spalding. From Spalding, follow the trail along the ridge to the summit of Mount Evans. Note: From Summit Lake, you will not gain the required 3,000 feet in altitude. The Colorado Fourteeners Initiative has built a route from Chicago Lakes basin to Summit Lake that provides hikers with a route that will give them the 3,000 feet of elevation gain. You may see mountain goats during the climb, especially below Summit Lake or on the Sawtooth Ridge between Mount Evans and Mount Bierstadt.

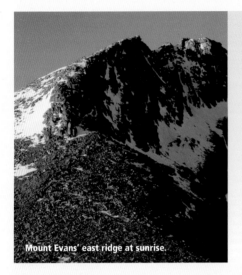

Mount Evans' east ridge at sunrise.

**HISTORY:** Once called "Mount Rosalie," the Colorado legislature renamed this peak "Mount Evans" in 1895 in honor of Colorado's second territorial governor. In addition to leadership roles with the Denver Pacific and the Denver, South Park, and Pacific railroads, John Evans was a benefactor of the University of Denver and an influential businessman.

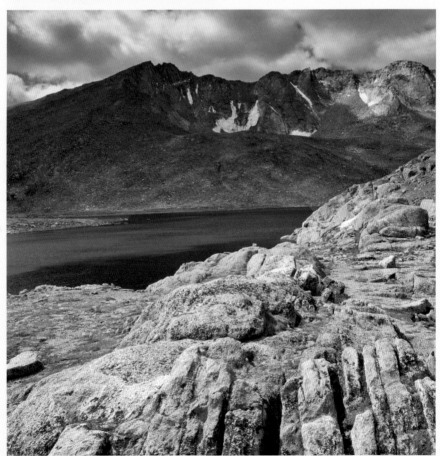

Mount Evans from the start of Mount Spalding's east ridge.

The view north from Mount Evans' summit.

## SIDEBAR: RIDE A FOURTEENER

The Bob Cook Memorial Mount Evans Hill Climb starts at 7,540 feet in front of the Clear Creek Middle School and climbs on the highest paved road in the United States to the Mount Evans summit over a 28-mile route.

# Mount Bierstadt
## 14,060 feet

| MAPS | Trails Illustrated 104–Idaho Springs/Georgetown/Loveland Pass; Mount Evans 7.5 minute |
|------|------|
| RATING | Moderate |
| ELEVATION GAIN | 2,400 feet |
| ROUND-TRIP DISTANCE | 6 miles |
| ROUND-TRIP TIME | 6 hours |
| NEAREST TOWN | Georgetown |
| RANGER DISTRICT | US Forest Service, South Platte Ranger District, 303-275-5610 |

**COMMENT:** The standard route starts at the Guanella Pass Trailhead. Both Mount Bierstadt and Mount Evans may be climbed in one day. However, the Sawtooth Ridge connecting the two mountains is exposed and is difficult if you are not a rock climber. Do not attempt this route unless you are confident of your abilities. Consult more detailed guides if you plan to do this traverse. Be especially watchful of the weather.

CFI completed trail construction and restoration work on this route in 1999–2002. Due to high use, this trail tends to get very wide and braided. Always stay on the main trail, do not cut switchbacks, and if you encounter very wide and/or braided sections of trail, hike single-file on the most eroded/impacted part of the trail to prevent further widening.

**GETTING THERE:** From Georgetown, drive south 11 miles along South Clear Creek Road to Guanella Pass at 11,669 feet. The peak is in view to the east-southeast.

**THE ROUTE:** Hike 1 mile on trail and boardwalk over the dreaded willows. The trail continues east, then south, to reach the west ridge of the peak. The trail then follows the ridge northeast to the summit.

Left. Mount Bierstadt from just below Mount Evans' summit.

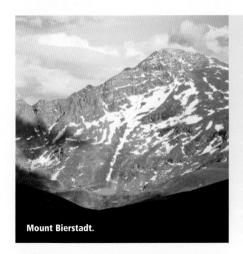

Mount Bierstadt.

**HISTORY:** Famed western landscape painter Albert Bierstadt was instrumental in originally naming Mount Evans "Mount Rosalie," after his future wife. In 1914, Ellsworth Bethel, the dean of Colorado mountain namers, firmly put Bierstadt's name on this summit—after it, too, had been called "Mount Rosalie" for a time.

Willows and tarns near Guanella Pass.

## SIDEBAR: **THE DREADED WILLOWS**

Before the boardwalk was built, the Bierstadt route worked its way through a willow swamp that was one of the worst approaches to any of the Fourteeners. There was no way to get through it with dry feet, and some idiot was always shouting, "Here's the way!" and he was always wrong.

# Pikes Peak
## 14,110 feet

| MAPS | Trails Illustrated 137–Pikes Peak/Canon City; Pikes Peak 7.5 minute |
| --- | --- |
| RATING | Moderate, but long |
| ELEVATION GAIN | 7,400 feet |
| ROUND-TRIP DISTANCE | 26 miles |
| ROUND-TRIP TIME | 12 to 14 hours |
| NEAREST TOWN | Manitou Springs |
| RANGER DISTRICT | US Forest Service, Pikes Peak Ranger District, 719-636-1602 |

**COMMENT:** This is a long hike. Before starting you may wish to inquire at the cog railroad about the possibility of taking the train down from the summit. Since there is a dirt road to the top of Pikes Peak, there is no register. The standard route is called the Barr Trail. You will find the Friends of the Peak (www.fotp.com) doing maintenance on the Barr Trail.

**GETTING THERE:** To reach the Barr Trail, drive to Manitou Springs and locate the city hall. Proceed west on US 25 (business) about 0.5 mile to Ruxton Avenue. Turn left on Ruxton Avenue and drive 0.75 mile to the Pikes Peak Cog Railroad depot, then on for a short distance to the hydroelectric plant and Hydro Street. Look for the Barr Trail parking lot and park there, if there is room.

**THE ROUTE:** From the south end of the parking lot, head up through switchbacks for 3 difficult miles to the top of the Manitou Incline. Ignore the mile markers, because they are wrong. Barr Camp is a relatively easy 3.5 miles from the top of the Incline. Take a break at the Barr Camp, where the trail gets steeper, moving up to an A-frame at about 12,000 feet. Follow the switchbacks to 12,800 feet, where the trail levels into a long traverse. Approximately 1 mile from the summit you will encounter the 16 Golden Stairs that you will always remember.

Left. Pikes Peak's north face in fall.

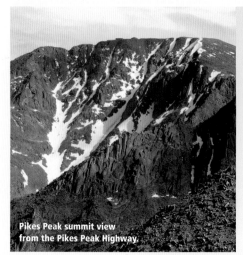

Pikes Peak summit view from the Pikes Peak Highway.

**HISTORY:** Lieutenant Zebulon Montgomery Pike explored the southern portion of the Louisiana Territory in 1806–07. In late November, Pike attempted to climb his "grand peak," but after two and a half days, he turned back, citing the existing winter conditions. Botanist Edwin James made the first recorded ascent on July 14, 1820.

Pikes Peak above timberline from Barr Trail.

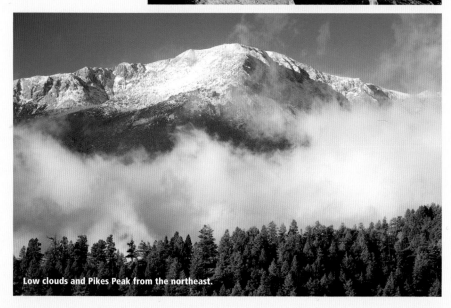

Low clouds and Pikes Peak from the northeast.

Kit Carson Peak from the summit of Hermit Peak, looking south.

# Kit Carson Peak
## 14,165 feet

| MAPS | Trails Illustrated 138–Sangre de Cristo Mountains; Crestone Peak 7.5 minute |
|---|---|
| RATING | Very difficult |
| ELEVATION GAIN | 2,500 feet from Willow Lake, 5,300 feet from the trailhead |
| ROUND-TRIP DISTANCE | 6 miles from Willow Lake, 13.5 miles from the trailhead |
| ROUND-TRIP TIME | 8 hours from Willow Lake |
| NEAREST TOWN | Crestone |
| RANGER DISTRICT | US Forest Service, Saguache Ranger District, 719-655-2547 |

**COMMENT:** Kit Carson Avenue is memorable. The standard route follows the Willow Lake Trail and then heads up the mountain's north slope. Kit Carson Peak is on the massif Kit Carson Mountain. Challenger Point and Columbia Point are also on Kit Carson Mountain.

**GETTING THERE:** Approaching from the north, go 14 miles on Colorado 17 from the junction of Colorado 17 and US 285, or, approaching from the south, go north 17 miles from Hooper on Colorado 17. From either direction, you next turn east on a paved road and travel 12.5 miles to Crestone. From Crestone, go east on Galena Street, reaching the trailhead after approximately 2 miles. From the Willow Creek Trailhead, hike approximately 7.5 miles to Willow Lake.

**THE ROUTE:** Take the trail around the north side of the lake and continue above the falls. It's a steep climb to Challenger Point. Over the point is the west side of Kit Carson, with a shelf called "Kit Carson Avenue." The Avenue leads around the west face of the peak and goes up the south side of the peak.

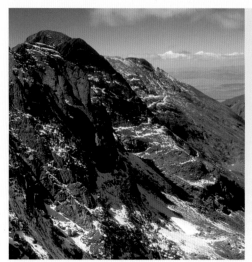

**HISTORY:** Kit Carson Peak takes its name from the famous scout who, in the mid-1860s, commanded Fort Garland at the base of Blanca Peak. In 1987, the 14,081-foot northwest sub-peak of Kit Carson was named Challenger Point, commemorating the crew members of the space shuttle Challenger, who lost their lives on January 28, 1986.

Kit Carson.                     PHOTO BY DAVID HITE

Telephoto view of Kit Carson Mountain (left to right): Challenger Point, Kit Carson Peak, and Columbia Point.

## SIDEBAR: **12,000-FOOT MANTRA**

After you pass 12,000 feet, the going will get tougher. It helps to repeat three or four words as a mountaineer's mantra. Here are a few of the words that will help get you up the route if mumbled over and over again between breaths: relentless, implacable, resolute, stubborn, undaunted, intrepid, headstrong, stalwart, tenacious, persistent, tireless, enduring.

We have used *relentless—enduring—stubborn—tenacious* with some success.

# Humboldt Peak

## 14,064 feet

| | |
|---|---|
| **MAPS** | Trails Illustrated 138–Sangre de Cristo Mountains; Crestone Peak 7.5 minute |
| **RATING** | Moderate |
| **ELEVATION GAIN** | 2,400 feet from lower South Colony Lake |
| **ROUND-TRIP DISTANCE** | 3.5 miles from lower South Colony Lake, 8.5 miles from the trailhead |
| **ROUND-TRIP TIME** | 5 hours from lower South Colony Lake |
| **NEAREST TOWN** | Westcliffe |
| **RANGER DISTRICT** | US Forest Service, San Carlos Ranger District, 719-269-8500 |

**COMMENT:** Of the four mountains in the "Crestones"—Crestone Peak, Crestone Needle, Kit Carson, and Humboldt—Humboldt is the easiest. The standard route is the South Colony Lake Route up to the saddle and east to the summit.

**GETTING THERE:** From Westcliffe, drive southeast about 4.5 miles on Colorado 69 toward Walsenburg. Turn right (south), go 5.5 miles to the end of Colfax Lane, then turn right again. You are now headed straight west toward the Crestones. After about 1 mile, the road becomes very rugged, but four-wheel-drive vehicles with good ground clearance can be driven up the road to a gate, where you will find a parking lot for 50 vehicles, and 20 designated camping sites. The lakes are about 4 miles from the gate and have designated camping sites.

**THE ROUTE:** From lower South Colony Lake, hike northwest on the trail up South Colony Creek to the east side of upper South Colony Lake. Follow the Humboldt Trail north up scree and talus to Humboldt's west ridge. Reach the ridge just east of the 12,850-foot connecting saddle between Humboldt and Crestone peaks. Climb east on the ridge for less than a mile to the summit.

Left. Humboldt Peak's west ridge from the North Colony–South Colony saddle.

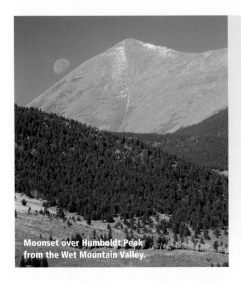

Moonset over Humboldt Peak from the Wet Mountain Valley.

**HISTORY:** This peak was named in honor of Alexander von Humboldt, an eminent German geographer and mountaineer who made an unsuccessful 1802 assault on Ecuador's Mount Chimborazo, then thought to be the highest peak in the world. Humboldt was officially climbed in 1883, but it is likely that miners reached the summit before that.

Sunset on (left to right) Crestone Needle (barely visible), Mount Adams, Crestone Peak, and Columbia/Kit Carson/Challenger, from the summit of Hermit Peak.

## SIDEBAR: **THE ROAD**

No one is kidding about this alleged road up to the Crestone Group. Even though it gets bladed every once in a while, it is usually awful. We high-centered a Subie station wagon on this "road," took an hour to get it off, then said the hell with it and drove up to do Belford and Oxford instead, where we were almost incinerated by lightning. It was a bad Fourteener day.

# Crestone Peak

## 14,294 feet

| | |
|---|---|
| **MAPS** | Trails Illustrated 138–Sangre de Cristo Mountains; Crestone Peak 7.5 minute |
| **RATING** | Very difficult |
| **ELEVATION GAIN** | 2,600 feet from lower South Colony Lake |
| **ROUND-TRIP DISTANCE** | 4 miles from lower South Colony Lake |
| **ROUND-TRIP TIME** | 8 hours from lower South Colony Lake, 12 hours from the trailhead |
| **NEAREST TOWN** | Westcliffe |
| **RANGER DISTRICT** | US Forest Service, San Carlos Ranger District, 719-269-8500 |

**COMMENT:** A climbing helmet, rope, and ice axe are highly recommended for this route. There is residual ice on the couloir near the summit well into the summer, and an ice axe may be required. Falling rock presents another hazard, making the use of a helmet a very good idea. Be careful. The standard route is from lower South Colony Lake up the south face.

**GETTING THERE:** From Westcliffe, drive southeast about 4.5 miles on Colorado 69 toward Walsenburg. Turn right (south), go 5.5 miles to the end of Colfax Lane, then turn right again. You are now headed straight west toward the Crestones. After about 1 mile, the road becomes very rugged, but four-wheel-drive vehicles with good ground clearance can be driven up the road to a gate, where you will find a parking lot for 50 vehicles, and 20 designated camping sites. The lakes are about 4 miles from the gate and have designated camping sites.

**THE ROUTE:** Circle lower South Colony Lake to the south and west. Climb southwest to the saddle between Crestone Needle and Broken Hand Peak. Drop down from Broken Hand Pass to the southwest and around Cottonwood Lake, moving in a westerly direction. Looking north, you will see the south face of Crestone Peak and the red couloir. The route follows the red couloir to a difficult summit.

Left. Crestone Peak and alpine avens on the Humboldt saddle, looking west.

Sunrise on Crestone Peak.

**HISTORY:** Rugged, isolated, and unforgiving, Crestone Peak dominates an area of the central Sangre de Cristo Range that until 1967 did not even have an adequate topographic map. The word *Crestone* is from the Spanish "cresta," meaning the top of a cock's comb or the crest of a helmet.

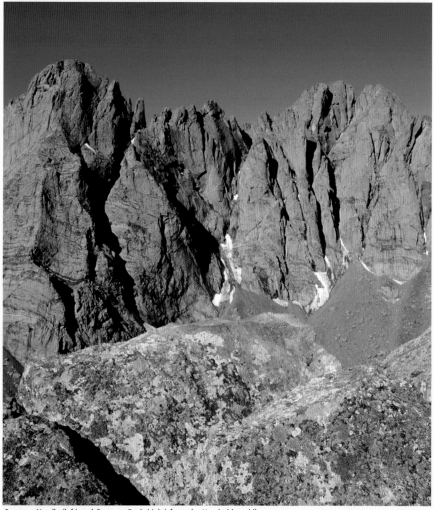

Crestone Needle (left) and Crestone Peak (right) from the Humboldt saddle.

# Crestone Needle

## 14,197 feet

| MAPS | Trails Illustrated 138–Sangre de Cristo Mountains; Crestone Peak 7.5 minute |
|---|---|
| RATING | Very difficult |
| ELEVATION GAIN | 2,500 feet from lower South Colony Lake, 4,000 feet from the trailhead |
| ROUND-TRIP DISTANCE | 3 miles from lower South Colony Lake, 5.5 miles from the trailhead |
| ROUND-TRIP TIME | 6 hours from lower South Colony Lake, 10 hours from the trailhead |
| NEAREST TOWN | Westcliffe |
| RANGER DISTRICT | US Forest Service, San Carlos Ranger District, 719-269-8500 |

**COMMENT:** This peak, once considered unclimbable, was the last of the Colorado Fourteeners to be summited. The various routes up the east face are technical climbs. Though it is a good precaution to carry a rope, the south face can, with care, be climbed unassisted. It goes without saying that a helmet should be worn on this route. The standard route is from lower South Colony Lake up the south face.

**GETTING THERE:** From Westcliffe, drive southeast about 4.5 miles on Colorado 69 toward Walsenburg. Turn right (south), go 5.5 miles to the end of Colfax Lane, then turn right again. You are now headed straight west toward the Crestones. After about 1 mile, the road becomes very rugged, but four-wheel-drive vehicles with good ground clearance can be driven up the road to a gate, where you will find a parking lot for 50 vehicles, and 20 designated camping sites. The lakes are about 4 miles from the gate, and have designated camping sites.

**THE ROUTE:** Circle lower South Colony Lake to the south and west. Climb southwest to the saddle between Crestone Needle and Broken Hand Peak. Continue northwest along the ridge toward the Needle. About 0.2 mile above the first bench, angle slightly right and look for a cairn-marked zigzag route on grass shelves. This route leads to the third pinnacle northeast of a low point on the ridge. Drop slightly

Left. The official turnoff along South Colony Creek for Crestone Needle's standard route.

into a narrow couloir and climb abruptly up to the summit. Look for a cairned route and follow it in your descent; otherwise, you may find yourself on a cliff overhang, and will have to climb back up or use a rope.

**HISTORY:** Crestone Needle was the last Colorado Fourteener to be climbed. Albert R. Ellingwood, grand master of early Colorado climbing, and Eleanor Davis, the first woman to climb all the Fourteeners, traversed below the spindly spires of the connecting ridge from Crestone Peak to reach the top on July 24, 1916.

Top.
Telephoto view of Broken Hand Pass.

Left.
Telephoto view of Crestone Needle and the start of the Needle-to-Peak connecting ridge.

Mount Lindsey from the west.

# Mount Lindsey
## 14,042 feet

| MAPS | Trails Illustrated 138–Sangre de Cristo Mountains; Mosca Pass 7.5 minute, Blanca Peak 7.5 minute |
|---|---|
| **RATING** | More difficult |
| **ELEVATION GAIN** | 3,400 feet |
| **ROUND-TRIP DISTANCE** | 8 miles |
| **ROUND-TRIP TIME** | 8 hours |
| **NEAREST TOWN** | Westcliffe |
| **RANGER DISTRICT** | US Forest Service, Conejos Ranger District, 719-271-8971 |

**COMMENT:** Finding your way to the trailhead is more difficult than following the climbing route. The standard climbing route is the Huerfano River Valley Route.

**GETTING THERE:** Two miles north of Walsenburg, Colorado 69 intersects Interstate 25 at exit 52. Take Colorado 69 for 25 miles to Gardner. Approximately 0.2 mile west of Gardner, take the left fork onto an unmarked county road. Drive for 13 miles, passing the town of Redwing. Take the left fork onto Forest Service Road 407 in the San Isabel National Forest and continue 4 miles to a sign identifying the private property of Singing River Ranch. Ranch owners do not permit parking or camping on their property. Please close all cattle gates as you traverse the ranch. The next 7 miles to the road's end can be rough, and are best suited for a four-wheel-drive vehicle. Park at the southwest end of the State Wildlife Area.

**THE ROUTE:** From the end of the road, hike 1.5 miles south on an old jeep road to the end of the marsh. Turn to the southeast and climb up the drainage to a large grassy basin west of the Iron Nipple. From the grassy basin, climb southeast under a ridge to the right. Ascend a gully before climbing up to the northwest end of the summit ridge. At approximately 13,400 feet, a cleft in the ridge offers difficulty over one short, steep point. Beyond that point this route is not difficult. The summit of Mount Lindsey is private property. Please be respectful.

**HISTORY:** Pioneers christened this peak "Old Baldy" for its denuded, round appearance from the San Luis Valley. At the request of the Colorado Mountain Club, this name was changed in 1953 to honor Malcolm Lindsey, a Colorado attorney who was a vital force in that organization's junior activities.

Top.
Mount Lindsey, looking southwest from the Wet Mountain valley.

Left.
Mount Lindsey from the east, along US 160.

# Little Bear Peak
## 14,037 feet

| MAPS | Trails Illustrated 138–Sangre de Cristo Mountains; Blanca Peak 7.5 minute, Twin Peaks 7.5 minute |
|---|---|
| RATING | Very difficult |
| ELEVATION GAIN | 2,300 feet from Lake Como |
| ROUND-TRIP DISTANCE | 4 miles from Lake Como |
| ROUND-TRIP TIME | 6.5 hours from Lake Como |
| NEAREST TOWN | Blanca |
| RANGER DISTRICT | US Forest Service, Conejos Ranger District, 719-271-8971 |

**COMMENT:** Steep slabs and falling rock make a helmet a "must-have" on this route. The standard route is the Como Lake Route up the west ridge. This is a dangerous climb. It is advisable to avoid crowds and put it up midweek.

**GETTING THERE:** From US 160, 6 miles west of Blanca and 15 miles east of Alamosa, drive north on Colorado 150 for 3 miles to a rough road going east. Take this road that becomes progressively rougher and can damage a car. We highly recommend a serious four-wheel-drive vehicle for this road. Drive as far as possible along this road, then pack in to Lake Como at 11,700 feet. Camp at the east end of the lake or higher, near timberline.

**THE ROUTE:** Continue for 0.3 mile past Lake Como on the jeep road. In the flats, head south to an obvious couloir that leads to Little Bear's west ridge. Take the ridge until it becomes steep and jagged. Turn right and contour for about 0.25 mile to a steep couloir that heads directly toward the summit. This is a difficult and dangerous summit. There is a route between Little Bear and Blanca that is considered to be the most difficult traverse between Fourteeners. Don't do it unless you are an experienced climber.

Left. Little Bear Peak from the south, with autumn cottonwoods.

63

Little Bear.

**HISTORY:** In 1888, Charles Fay and J. R. Edmands set out to climb Blanca Peak, but ended up on what was then called West Peak. By this error, they made the first ascent of what came to be called Little Bear. Between Little Bear and Blanca lay a narrow ridge that Franklin Rhoda described as being "perfectly impassable to man."

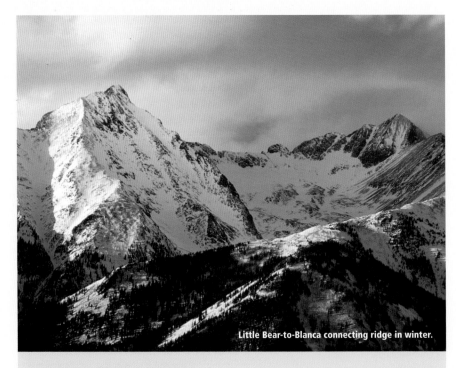

Little Bear-to-Blanca connecting ridge in winter.

## SIDEBAR: REALLY STUPID?

There are few climbers who have summited every mountain that they have attempted. There are myriad reasons for not completing a route. There is no dishonor in a reasoned decision to turn around and go down. The mountain will always be there to attempt again. There is a simple question to ask yourself in deciding whether or not to stop and go down. The question is, "Is what I'm doing really stupid?"

Little Bear Peak from Ellingwood Point.

PHOTO BY BILL MIDDLEBROOK

# Blanca Peak 14,345 feet
# Ellingwood Point 14,042 feet

| MAPS | Trails Illustrated 138–Sangre de Cristo Mountains; Blanca Peak 7.5 minute, Twin Peaks 7.5 minute |
| --- | --- |
| RATING | Moderate |
| ELEVATION GAIN | 3,200 feet, plus you lose and regain 1,000 feet on the traverse |
| ROUND-TRIP DISTANCE | 8 miles |
| ROUND-TRIP TIME | 8 hours |
| NEAREST TOWN | Blanca |
| RANGER DISTRICT | US Forest Service, Conejos Ranger District, 719-271-8971 |

COMMENT: Blanca and Ellingwood are traditionally done together. Done separately, the round-trip time for each mountain is 6 hours and the distance is 6 miles. The Como Lake Route up to the northeast is the standard route.

GETTING THERE: From US 160, 6 miles west of Blanca and 15 miles east of Alamosa, drive north on Colorado 150 for 3 miles to a rough road going east. Take this road that becomes progressively rougher and can damage a car. We highly recommend a serious four-wheel-drive vehicle for this road. Drive as far as possible along this road, then pack into Lake Como at 11,700 feet. Camp at the east end of the lake or higher, near timberline.

THE ROUTE: Hike northeast up the basin, passing north of Crater Lake, toward the Blanca-Ellingwood ridge. Halfway up to the ridge, turn right (south) to ascend Blanca, or left to reach Ellingwood. Return to the saddle to descend.

Left. Blanca Peak's north face from the Huerfano River valley.

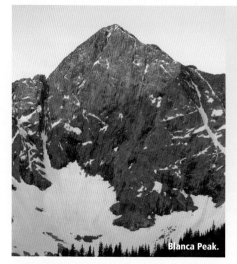

Blanca Peak.

**HISTORY:** Long a landmark, Blanca Peak has watched the march of the Ute, Spanish, and Anglo cultures across the San Luis Valley. *Blanca* means "white" in Spanish, and the mountain appears white most of the year—either because of snow or glistening rock. Blanca's western sub-peak is named for climber Albert Ellingwood.

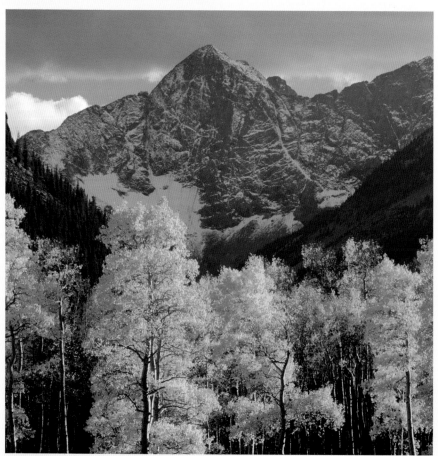

Blanca Peak's north face, as seen from the Huerfano River valley.

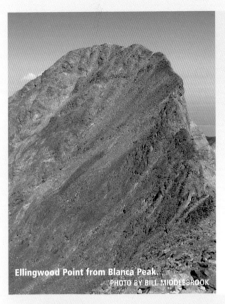

Ellingwood Point from Blanca Peak.
PHOTO BY BILL MIDDLEBROOK

## SIDEBAR: CELL PHONES

Take one with you. Turn it off. Cell phones don't work in the valleys and on approaches, but they sometimes work at altitude. There is always a fool on the summit attempting to talk to a significant other who probably doesn't give a damn.

A cell phone is a radio. If there is an emergency, use your map or GPS (if you have one) to identify the location (longitude and latitude or UTM coordinates) of the incident and call 911. If your cell doesn't acquire a signal, keep going higher, and keep trying.

# Culebra Peak
## 14,047 feet

| MAPS | Culebra Peak 7.5 minute, El Valle Creek 7.5 minute. There is no Trails Illustrated map for this peak. |
|---|---|
| RATING | Moderate |
| ELEVATION GAIN | 3,000 feet |
| ROUND-TRIP DISTANCE | 6.5 miles from the four-way intersection |
| ROUND-TRIP TIME | 6 hours |
| NEAREST TOWN | San Luis |
| CONTACT | Cielo Vista Ranch, 254-897-7872 |

**COMMENT:** Access to Culebra is restricted. Reservations are available by calling 254-897-7872. The fee is $100 and the Cielo Vista Ranch is open from the end of June to the end of August. The standard route is the northwest ridge route.

**GETTING THERE:** From San Luis, drive south and southeast on Colorado 152 through the town of Chama. The road turns east and is paved for 4 miles beyond Chama, where it crosses two bridges that are a few hundred feet apart. Immediately past the second bridge, make a sharp right turn and follow the dirt road about 1 mile to where the road ends at a "T" junction. Turn left, then continue to bear right and drive 2 miles more. Cielo Vista Ranch will be on your left. At the ranch you will be asked to pay the fee and sign a waiver, and you will be given a map.

**THE ROUTE:** After leaving the ranch, keep right at the first junction, then take the center fork where the road branches at timberline at a four-way intersection. Follow this road to where it crosses the creek. Ascend the ridge at the low point to the east. Follow the ridge south, then southeast. Culebra's summit becomes visible at the highest point south of the ridge. Continue south, then southeast, on the ridge. There is a small loss in elevation and some rock scrambling near the summit.

Left. Heading toward Culebra Peak's summit.

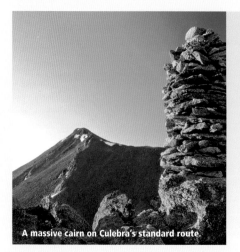

A massive cairn on Culebra's standard route.

**HISTORY:** The southernmost Fourteener in Colorado, Culebra misses being the highest point in New Mexico by less than ten miles. The mountain sits on private property on the remnants of old Spanish land grants. Its name is Spanish for "snake." Spanish explorers or land grant surveyors may have made the first ascent.

Culebra's summit (left) and false summit (right).

Looking northwest from Beaver Ridge to Quandary Peak.

# Quandary Peak
## 14,265 feet

| MAPS | Trails Illustrated 109–Breckenridge/Tennessee Pass; Breckenridge 7.5 minute |
| --- | --- |
| RATING | Moderate |
| ELEVATION GAIN | 3,300 feet |
| ROUND-TRIP DISTANCE | 6 miles |
| ROUND-TRIP TIME | 6 hours |
| NEAREST TOWN | Breckenridge |
| RANGER DISTRICT | US Forest Service, Dillon Ranger District, 970-468-5400 |

**COMMENT:** The route up and down Quandary is a favorite for back-country skiers. The Quandary Peak Route up the east ridge is the standard route.

CFI completed trail construction and restoration work on this peak in 2001–2002.

**GETTING THERE:** Drive west through the Eisenhower Tunnel on Interstate 70 and exit at Frisco, heading south on Colorado 9 toward Breckenridge. Continue south past the town for approximately 9 miles to where Colorado 9 starts to climb to Hoosier Pass. Make a right on Blue Lakes Road, marked as 850 (with a sign that looks like a street sign). You will be heading west up a canyon. Immediately thereafter, an unimproved road angles up to the right from County Road 850. Take McCullough Gulch Road (County Road 851) to a new trailhead and parking lot 0.1 mile from County Road 850.

**THE ROUTE:** The new trail is across the road and leads west through timber. Near tree line, the trail follows the south side of the long east ridge of the peak. At about 12,900 feet, the trail joins the main ridge and continues over tundra and talus to the summit.

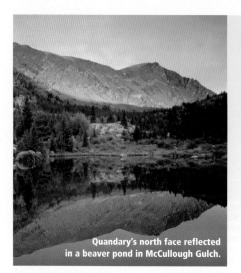

Quandary's north face reflected in a beaver pond in McCullough Gulch.

**HISTORY:** Quandary Peak reportedly gets its name from miners who were in a quandary over the proper identification of a mineral specimen found on its slopes. The fact that the peak was variously referred to as McCullough's Peak, Ute Peak, and Hoosier Peak may have left just about everyone in a quandary as to its name.

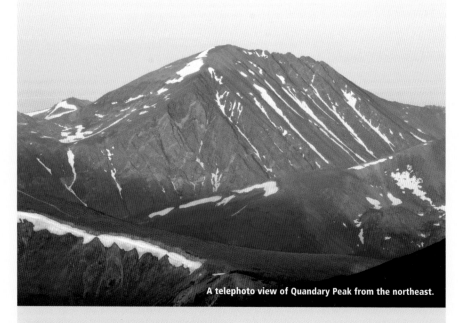

A telephoto view of Quandary Peak from the northeast.

## SIDEBAR: A DAY TO ACCLIMATE

If you are coming from the flatlands to do a Fourteener, give yourself a break and spend 24 hours or so in a mountain town relaxing before you put-up a route. Go for a real easy run, drink a good deal of water, and avoid alcohol—it is a depressant, something you don't need in your system when you are climbing. We're not kidding about the alcohol; wait till you come down from the climb.

Mount Democrat at sunset rises above an unnamed lake east of Mount Arkansas.

# Mount Democrat 14,148 feet
# Mount Lincoln 14,286 feet
# Mount Bross 14,172 feet

| MAPS | Trails Illustrated 109–Breckenridge/Tennessee Pass; Alma 7.5 minute, Climax 7.5 minute |
|---|---|
| RATING | Moderate |
| ELEVATION GAIN | 3,300 feet (lose and gain 700 feet between Democrat and Lincoln, lose and gain 600 feet between Lincoln and Bross) |
| ROUND-TRIP DISTANCE | 6 miles |
| ROUND-TRIP TIME | 8 hours |
| NEAREST TOWN | Alma |
| RANGER DISTRICT | US Forest Service, South Park Ranger District, 719-836-2031 |

COMMENT: The standard route is the Kite Lake Route, which is a loop that goes up to Mount Democrat, then to Mount Cameron, Mount Lincoln, and below the summit of Mount Bross before returning to Kite Lake. This loop makes for a long day.

As of 2009, access has been granted by private landowners to Mount Democrat and Mount Lincoln (as well as over the sub-peak, Cameron). The summit of Mount Bross remains closed to public access, although you can still complete the full trail loop skirting beneath the summit of Bross.

CFI has partnered with local landowners, CMC, Mosquito Range Heritage Initiative, and the US Forest Service to regain access to these mountains (all of these summits were closed to public access in 2006 until early 2009). Those of us at CFI and CMC cannot stress enough how important it is that you stay on the trail at all times, respect trail signage, stay off of closed routes, and stay away from old mines and mine structures. The 2009 reopening of access to Democrat and Lincoln is a CONDITIONAL reopening based upon your observance of the rules now, and in the future.

GETTING THERE: Drive on US 285 to Fairplay, then north on Colorado 9 for 6 miles to Alma. In the center of town, turn left (west) and drive 3 miles up Buckskin Creek Road (also called Secondary Forest Route 416) to Kite Lake.

**THE ROUTE:** From Kite Lake, follow the trail north 2 miles to the saddle. Climb Democrat 0.5 mile to the southwest. Return to the saddle and climb northeast for another 0.5 mile over Mount Cameron, and then an easy 0.5 mile to the summit of Mount Lincoln. Return to the Mount Cameron-Lincoln saddle and follow the gentle trail southeast 1 mile to Mount Bross. Return to Kite Lake for 1.5 miles down the west slope of Bross, taking the trail along the ridge. Continue down a couloir to the old road and back to the lake.

**HISTORY:** In 1861, Wilbur F. Stone, who later helped draft Colorado's Constitution, climbed the highest summit west of Hoosier Pass and suggested that it be named in honor of the recently elected president of the United States, Abraham Lincoln, a Republican. Naturally, there also had to be a Mount Democrat. Mount Bross was named for William Bross, a lieutenant governor of Illinois, who owned mining property near Alma.

Mount Lincoln at sunrise from near the summit of Mount Bross, looking north. (Quandary rises beyond.)

The west slopes of Mount Bross reflect in a rocky tarn above Lake Emma.

# Mount Sherman
## 14,036 feet

| MAPS | Trails Illustrated 110–Leadville/Fairplay; Mount Sherman 7.5 minute |
|---|---|
| RATING | Moderate |
| ELEVATION GAIN | 2,400 feet |
| ROUND-TRIP DISTANCE | 6 miles |
| ROUND-TRIP TIME | 8 hours |
| NEAREST TOWN | Fairplay |
| RANGER DISTRICT | US Forest Service, South Park Ranger District, 719-836-2031 |

**COMMENT:** For a more interesting trip, you can climb Mount Sheridan (13,768 feet) first, then drop to the saddle and continue up the long ridge to the summit of Mount Sherman. The standard route is the Fourmile Creek Route. The Day Mine Company of Leadville, which permits climbers to go through its property to the summit, owns the entire mountain.

**GETTING THERE:** Drive on US 285 to Fairplay, then continue south past the town for about 1 mile. Turn west (right) on Park County Road 18 (also called 4 Mile Creek Road) to Fourmile Creek. Drive 10 miles to the site of Leavick, a ghost town. Continue 2 miles and park below a gate at 12,000 feet. Park here and find a campsite in the environs, if you plan to camp.

**THE ROUTE:** Begin hiking on the road and pass the first mine, the Dauntless. Hike northwest up the most obvious road to the abandoned Hilltop Mine, then follow a trail up to the saddle between Mount Sheridan and Mount Sherman. Turn north (right) and hike up the ridge about 1 mile to the summit of Mount Sherman.

Left. The west slopes of Mount Sherman, viewed from Iowa Gulch.

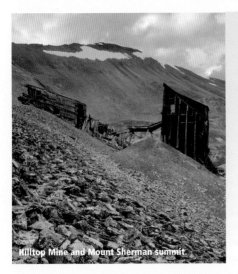

Hilltop Mine and Mount Sherman summit.

**HISTORY:** Mount Sherman's namesake is probably Civil War general William Tecumseh Sherman. As in the rest of the Mosquito Range, mining activity on the mountain was frenzied, and a first ascent by miners in the 1860s is almost a certainty. In 1967, a Cessna 310 made an emergency landing on its broad summit plateau.

Dauntless Mine and Mount Sherman summit.

## SIDEBAR: **TRAIL RIGHT-OF-WAY**

The person coming downhill has the right-of-way, because it is often easier to stop and step aside when you are going uphill than it is when you are going downhill.

# Mount of the Holy Cross
## 14,005 feet

| MAPS | Trails Illustrated 126–Holy Cross/Ruedi Reservoir; Holy Cross 7.5 minute, Minturn 7.5 minute |
| --- | --- |
| RATING | Moderate, but long |
| ELEVATION GAIN | 3,700 feet, plus you lose and gain 960 feet on Half Moon pass |
| ROUND-TRIP DISTANCE | 14 miles |
| ROUND-TRIP TIME | 12 hours |
| NEAREST TOWN | Minturn |
| RANGER DISTRICT | US Forest Service, Holy Cross Ranger District, 970-827-5715 |

**COMMENT:** When you review this route on your map, note that this is one of those routes, like the Barr Trail on Pikes Peak, where you lose altitude on the approach—in this case, almost 1,000 feet—that you gain and then lose and then have to gain again. On the way back down to your car, you have to climb back up Half Moon Pass. It can make you a tad bit grumpy. The Half Moon Pass Route is the standard route. Every year, a number of climbers get lost on this route and call the Forest Service or local sheriff for help. Take a map and compass. You have been warned.

CFI Adopt-a-Peak groups have been doing trail maintenance on Mount of the Holy Cross since 2006, and more intensive work is slated for the next few years to reroute and restore badly-eroding sections of trail. Please note that the Forest Service is highly concerned about camping in the East Cross Creek valley.

The issue with camping is that a number of goatheads have taken a dump and not buried it, that or they camped too close to the lake. If you can, hike Mount of the Holy Cross in one full day to minimize further camping impacts. If you do choose to camp in the East Cross Creek valley, remember to camp at least 200 feet away from the stream, and dig a cat hole 6–8 inches deep, and at least 200 feet away from water and campsites ... or better yet, pack it out in sanitary bags (human waste bags are available at most outdoor retailer stores).

**GETTING THERE:** From Minturn, drive south on US 24 for 3 miles, then turn right (southwest) and drive on Forest Service Road 701 for 8.5 miles, passing Tigiwon Campground, to Halfmoon Campground at 10,300 feet. Camp in this area.

**THE ROUTE:** Hike west 2 miles to Half Moon Pass at 11,600 feet. Descend 1.7 miles and 960 feet to East Cross Creek. Follow the trail west around a small lake 0.5 mile to the ridge and bear south up the ridge for 3 miles to the summit. Be careful on the descent not to drop left (west) into the West Cross Creek drainage. Remain on the north ridge of the mountain until the trail used during the ascent can be clearly identified descending into the trees at timberline.

**HISTORY:** Early reports of a mountain with a cross may have referred to seams of quartz near Fletcher Mountain. The snowy cross shape on the Mount of the Holy Cross was first officially reported in 1869, when it was seen from the summit of Grays Peak. In 1873, William Henry Jackson photographed the cross, while two other Hayden Survey members made the first ascent of the mountain.

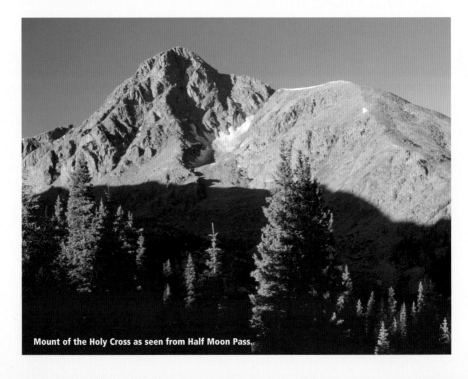

Mount of the Holy Cross as seen from Half Moon Pass.

# Mount Massive

## 14,421 feet

| MAPS | Trails Illustrated 127–Aspen/Independence Pass; Mount Massive 7.5 minute |
|---|---|
| RATING | Moderate |
| ELEVATION GAIN | 4,400 feet |
| ROUND-TRIP DISTANCE | 13.5 miles |
| ROUND-TRIP TIME | 10 hours |
| NEAREST TOWN | Leadville |
| RANGER DISTRICT | US Forest Service, Leadville Ranger District, 719-486-0749 |

**COMMENT:** This route along a segment of the Colorado Trail and up the east side of Massive is one of the more beautiful Fourteener trails. The standard route is the Mount Massive Trail Route.

CFI completed trail construction and restoration work on this route in 2006–2009. Be sure to stay on the standard route. Alpine plants take many years to reestablish—you can help by staying off of closed trails.

**GETTING THERE:** From Malta Junction, which is about 3 miles southwest of Leadville on US 24, drive west on County Road 300 for 1 mile, then head south on Forest Road 110 for 5.5 miles to Halfmoon Campground at 10,000 feet. Camp here, or proceed another 1.5 miles west and park at the Mount Massive parking lot, where the Colorado Trail crosses the road. You can also park at the Mount Massive overflow lot on the left.

**THE ROUTE:** Take the Colorado Trail north 3 miles to the Mount Massive Trail. Follow this trail through timber, then into a bowl and onto the northeast shoulder of the summit. This trail takes you very close to the summit, but some boulder scrambling is required near the top.

Left. Looking southwest over Native Lake toward Mount Massive.

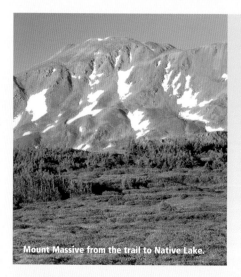

Mount Massive from the trail to Native Lake.

**HISTORY:** With five main points above 14,000 feet and a broad three-mile summit crest, there's really no other name for it. Henry Gannett climbed, named, and mapped the mountain for the Hayden Survey in 1873. Local sentiment in Leadville has preserved the name despite outside attempts to change it to McKinley, Gannett, or Churchill.

Moonset over a snow-covered Mount Massive.

## SIDEBAR: BOOTS

It goes without saying that the boots you use on a Fourteener should be broken in. We have used everything from heavy, leather, steel-shanked mountaineering boots to trail running shoes. The old waffle stompers were just too heavy. The trail running shoes were ultralight, but offered no protection at all. We have compromised with high-topped, lightweight hiking boots made out of few discernable natural materials. These boots are light and tough, and they offer some protection, provide decent support, and have an aggressive tread pattern.

Mount Elbert in winter, as viewed from the northeast near Leadville.

# Mount Elbert
## 14,433 feet

| MAPS | Trails Illustrated 127–Aspen/Independence Pass, Mount Elbert 7.5 minute |
|---|---|
| RATING | Moderate |
| ELEVATION GAIN | 4,400 feet from Halfmoon Creek |
| ROUND-TRIP DISTANCE | 10 miles from Halfmoon Creek |
| ROUND-TRIP TIME | 9 hours from Halfmoon Creek |
| NEAREST TOWN | Leadville |
| RANGER DISTRICT | US Forest Service, Leadville Ranger District, 719-486-0749 |

**COMMENT:** Mount Elbert is not a particularly striking mountain and the route is a walk-up, but Elbert is the highest Fourteener. There are two standard routes, the Halfmoon Creek Route (North Mount Elbert Trail) and the Mount Elbert Trail (South Mount Elbert Trail).

The US Forest Service completed trail construction and restoration work in 1994.

**GETTING THERE:** To get to North Mount Elbert Trail, from Malta Junction, which is about 3 miles southwest of Leadville on US 24, drive west on County Road 300 for 1 mile, then head south on Forest Road 110 for 5.5 miles to Halfmoon Campground at 10,000 feet. Camp here, or proceed another 1.5 miles west and park where the Colorado Trail crosses the road. There is a large parking lot on the left and a sign for the Mt. Elbert Trailhead. There are also outhouses.

**THE ROUTE:** Hike south on the Colorado Trail for 2 miles to a well-defined fork in the trail. Turn right (west) at the fork and climb 3 miles up a rather steep trail (southwest) to the summit.

**ALTERNATE ROUTE:** From Colorado 82, take Lake County Road 24. Pass Lakeview and continue for 0.3 mile more. Take an unmarked road straight ahead where Road 24 turns right. Continue on for about 2 miles and park. Hike west on a rough road that becomes a trail. The trail connects with the Colorado Trail. Watch for a sign for the Mount Elbert Trail that will take you to the summit. This trail is in need of repair and has a steep and confusing start. It is also braided and eroded. To prevent further braiding and widening by hiking, stay on the most impacted trail.

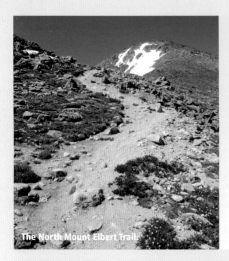

The North Mount Elbert Trail.

**HISTORY:** Mount Elbert was named for Samuel Elbert, who came to Colorado in 1862 as secretary to Territorial Governor John Evans. Elbert furthered his political fortunes by marrying Evans' daughter, Josephine, in 1865. After his own tenure as territorial governor, Elbert served twenty years on the state supreme court.

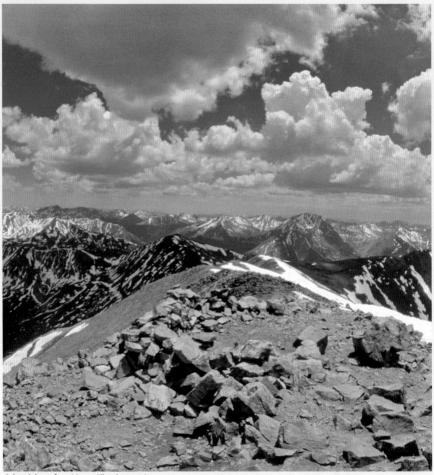

Colorado's rooftop, Mount Elbert's summit.

Sunset on La Plata Peak from Independence Pass, looking east-southeast.

# La Plata Peak

## 14,336 feet

| MAPS | Trails Illustrated 127–Aspen/Independence Pass; Winfield 7.5 minute, Mount Elbert 7.5 minute |
|---|---|
| RATING | More difficult |
| ELEVATION GAIN | 4,100 feet |
| ROUND-TRIP DISTANCE | 10 miles |
| ROUND-TRIP TIME | 9 hours |
| NEAREST TOWN | Leadville |
| RANGER DISTRICT | US Forest Service, Leadville Ranger District, 719-486-0749 |

**COMMENT:** There are a number of braided trails on this route. Please stay on the designated trail marked by cairns. The Northwest Ridge is the standard route.

CFI completed route construction work in 1995.

**GETTING THERE:** From Leadville, drive toward Independence Pass on US 24, then turn west (right) onto Colorado 82. Continue for 14.5 miles. Look for a parking area on your left near the South Fork Lake Creek Road.

**THE ROUTE:** Hike along South Fork Lake Creek Road, crossing Lake Creek on a bridge, and follow signs to the trailhead. The standard route is to the west of the trail marked on the USGS quad. The first mile of the climb passes through private property. Continue through forest and meadow to the east of the ridge. Traverse south under the ridge and follow a couloir to the southeast and then up the west side of the peak. As you are approaching the ridgeline/saddle at about 12,700 feet, watch carefully for the correct trail route. Follow the rock steps and rubble walls to guide you up to this section, and do not veer right (south) into the closed restoration area. Be careful of the same on your return route. Watch along the ridgeline to the summit for occasional cairns that will keep you on-route and off of restoration areas.

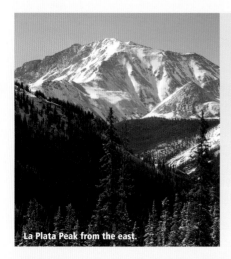

La Plata Peak from the east.

**HISTORY:** La Plata was probably first climbed by miners in the late 1860s or early 1870s. Numerous silver mines dot its upper slopes, particularly above the mining camps of Vicksburg and Winfield. Hayden Survey members made La Plata's first recorded ascent on July 26, 1873. They gave the peak its name, which means "silver" in Spanish.

La Plata Peak, looking north from near Browns Peak's summit.

## SIDEBAR: **WHEN YOU ARE FEELING PUKEY**

Acute Mountain Sickness (AMS) can strike just about anyone at any time, at altitude. We've had flatlander friends get sick on the ride up Interstate 70 at 8,000 feet, and we've all, at one time or another, gotten AMS at different altitudes. It is simply hard to predict who will get it, or when. Apparently, getting AMS is related to your physiology; some people can go from sea level to 14,000 feet with no ill effects at all, and some highly trained individuals get sick at 10,000 feet.

The symptoms of AMS are headache, nausea, loss of appetite, fatigue, dizziness, and sometimes vomiting.

Mount Oxford (left) and Mount Belford (right) from the north, looking across the Clear Creek valley.

# Mount Belford 14,197 feet
# Mount Oxford 14,153 feet

| | |
|---|---|
| **MAPS** | Trails Illustrated 129–Buena Vista/Collegiate Peaks; Mount Harvard 7.5 minute |
| **RATING** | Moderate |
| **ELEVATION GAIN** | 4,600 feet, plus you lose and regain 700 feet in the saddle in each direction |
| **ROUND-TRIP DISTANCE** | 9 miles |
| **ROUND-TRIP TIME** | 10 hours |
| **NEAREST TOWN** | Buena Vista |
| **RANGER DISTRICT** | (Not available ) |

**COMMENT:** These two peaks are traditionally climbed together. The route between Belford and Oxford entails high altitude and exposure to whatever storms are lurking as you hike about a mile in each direction. Check the weather before proceeding, since there is no shelter from sudden storms. These two peaks have a well-deserved reputation for sudden, violent electrical storms. Climb them early in the morning. The standard route is the Missouri Gulch Route to Belford and then the saddle to Oxford.

CFI completed trail construction and restoration work in 1995–1996.

**GETTING THERE:** From Buena Vista, drive north on US 24 for 15 miles, turn left (west) on a gravel road running along the north side of the Clear Creek Reservoir, then proceed 8 miles to the ghost town of Vicksburg at 9,700 feet. There are small and primitive camp areas along Clear Creek, east and west of Vicksburg.

**THE ROUTE:** Cross Clear Creek on a bridge at Vicksburg and hike south on a trail up Missouri Gulch for 2 miles, then continue along the creek until you reach timberline. You will see the route up Belford's northwest shoulder. Continue on the Missouri Gulch trail to the trail junction at 11,650 feet. Take the left fork. The route climbs to the summit along a well-constructed trail. From the summit of Belford, find the trail that descends into the saddle between Belford and Oxford, dropping 700 feet. Watch the weather. Turn around if it looks at all bad. Continue east-northeast to Oxford. To descend, return to the saddle between Oxford and Belford. Return to Belford's summit via the same route. Descend using the ascent route.

**HISTORY:** James B. Belford was Colorado's first congressman and a powerful voice for the free coinage of silver. Belford's flaming red hair and fiery oratory earned him the nickname "the Red-Headed Rooster of the Rockies." In keeping with Collegiate Peaks' tradition, John L. Jerome Hart named Mount Oxford after the university he attended.

Top.
Waverly Mountain (left) and Mount Oxford (right) from near Quail Mount, looking south.

Left.
Mount Oxford (left) and Mount Belford (right) from the north, looking across the Clear Creek valley.

A tumbling creek below Missouri Mountain, looking south in Missouri Gulch.

# Missouri Mountain
## 14,067 feet

| MAPS | Trails Illustrated 129–Buena Vista/Collegiate Peaks; Winfield 7.5 minute |
| --- | --- |
| RATING | More difficult |
| ELEVATION GAIN | 4,500 feet |
| ROUND-TRIP DISTANCE | 9 miles |
| ROUND-TRIP TIME | 8 hours |
| NEAREST TOWN | Buena Vista |
| RANGER DISTRICT | US Forest Service, Leadville Ranger District, 719-486-0749 |

**COMMENT:** Be careful—Missouri Mountain can be a little more dangerous than you would expect. The Missouri Gulch Route to the northwest ridge is the standard route.

CFI completed trail construction and restoration work in 2000–2001.

**GETTING THERE:** From Buena Vista, drive north on US 24 for 15 miles, turn left (west) on a gravel road running along the north side of the Clear Creek Reservoir, then proceed 8 miles to the ghost town of Vicksburg at 9,700 feet. There are small and primitive camp areas along Clear Creek, east and west of Vicksburg.

**THE ROUTE:** Cross Clear Creek on the bridge at Vicksburg and hike south on the trail up Missouri Gulch for 3 miles to the head of the gulch, staying to the right at the trail junction at 11,650 feet. Take the trail west up the tundra slopes and across a talus field to a saddle on the ridge. Do not take the trail that heads east toward the rocks in the vicinity of Elkhead Pass, since this is a dangerous way to the summit. Once on the ridge, proceed south, then southeast, along the narrow ridge trail to the summit. There is some exposure along the ridge trail.

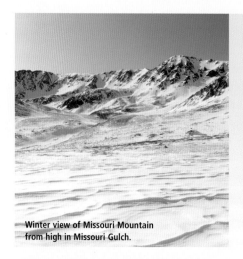

Winter view of Missouri Mountain from high in Missouri Gulch.

**HISTORY:** During the silver boom of the 1880s, miners roamed the Clear Creek valley to the north of Missouri Mountain. Miners from Missouri decided to show locals their fondness for the folks back home. They named Missouri Gulch, Missouri Basin, and Missouri Mountain and probably made the mountain's first ascent.

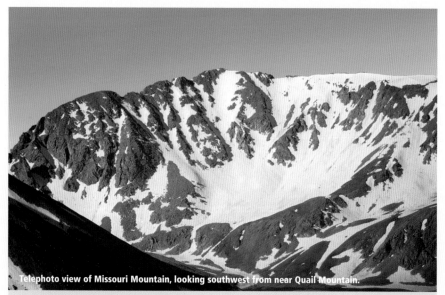

Telephoto view of Missouri Mountain, looking southwest from near Quail Mountain.

## SIDEBAR: SUMMIT TIME

Don't be surprised, on reaching the summit of a Fourteener, to find fifty or so other climbers sprawled all over the rocks.

The very first thing you should do when you summit is look around 360 degrees for a thunderstorm. Next, check that everyone in your crowd is feeling okay, then sit down for a snack and rehydration.

We have spent as little time on the summit as it takes to sign the register and beat feet downhill in front of a thunderstorm, and we have also lollygagged for an hour or so at 14,000 feet.

Stormy evening reflection of Huron Peak, looking northeast from Harrison Flat.

# Huron Peak

## 14,003 feet

| MAPS | Trails Illustrated 129–Buena Vista/Collegiate Peaks; Winfield 7.5 minute |
|---|---|
| RATING | Moderate |
| ELEVATION GAIN | 3,200 feet |
| ROUND-TRIP DISTANCE | 8.5 miles |
| ROUND-TRIP TIME | 6.5 hours |
| NEAREST TOWN | Buena Vista |
| RANGER DISTRICT | US Forest Service, Leadville Ranger District, 719-486-0749 |

**COMMENT:** The folks at the Colorado Fourteeners Initiative think Huron is one of the best viewing summits in the Sawatch Range. The North Ridge from Clear Creek is the standard route.

CFI completed trail construction and restoration work in 1998 and 2001.

**GETTING THERE:** From Buena Vista, drive north on US 24 for 15 miles, turn left (west) on a gravel road running along the north side of the Clear Creek Reservoir, then go about 12 miles, driving through the ghost towns of Vicksburg and Winfield. Turn left at Winfield and drive just over 2 miles past Winfield on the rough South Fork Clear Creek Road to the trailhead. Leave your vehicle there.

**THE ROUTE:** The Huron Peak Trail is on the left of the parking lot. Follow the trail to a small creek, then cross the creek and continue up numerous switchbacks to the timberline at about 11,800 feet. Stay on the trail through a large grassy basin and gain the saddle between Huron and Browns Peak, which can be seen to the north. Ascend Huron's northern rocky ridge. The Colorado Fourteeners Initiative has done significant maintenance on Huron to reclaim the heavily eroded slopes. Stay on the ridge and follow the well-marked and cairned route to the summit. Avoid the large scree and talus bowl. Remain on the ridge for the descent and follow Huron Peak Trail back to your vehicle.

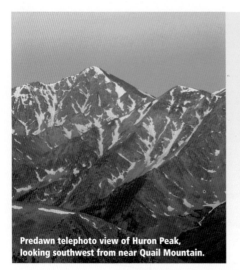

Predawn telephoto view of Huron Peak, looking southwest from near Quail Mountain.

**HISTORY:** Huron Peak was probably first climbed by miners. The exact origin of Huron's name is unknown, but it was probably named for a Huron mine somewhere in the vicinity. Huron was a relative latecomer to the Fourteener ranks and was not given official US Geological Survey designation above 14,000 feet until 1956.

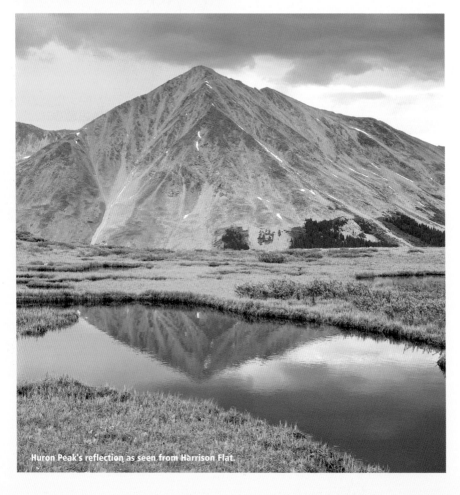

Huron Peak's reflection as seen from Harrison Flat.

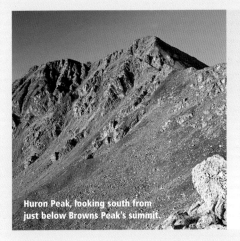

Huron Peak, looking south from just below Browns Peak's summit.

## SIDEBAR: THAT GURGLING SOUND

If, when breathing heavily at altitude, you hear a gurgling sound in your lungs ... STOP and immediately go downhill; you have symptoms of High Altitude Pulmonary Edema (HAPE). Other symptoms are shallow breathing, fatigue, and breathlessness while resting.

Mount Columbia, looking south along Frenchman Creek.

# Mount Harvard 14,420 feet
# Mount Columbia 14,073 feet

| | |
|---|---|
| MAPS | Trails Illustrated 129–Buena Vista/Collegiate Peaks; Mount Harvard 7.5 minute |
| RATING | More difficult |
| ELEVATION GAIN | 4,500 feet, plus you lose and gain 1,800 feet between Harvard and Columbia in each direction |
| ROUND-TRIP DISTANCE | 12 miles from Horn Fork Basin camp |
| ROUND-TRIP TIME | 12 hours from Horn Fork Basin camp |
| NEAREST TOWN | Buena Vista |
| RANGER DISTRICT | US Forest Service, Leadville Ranger District, 719-486-0749 |

**COMMENT:** It is traditional to do both Harvard and Columbia on the same day, if weather permits. The standard route is the Horn Fork Basin Route up the south ridge of Harvard and then to the southeast and south to Columbia. Avoid the ridge between Harvard and Columbia when thunderstorms are anywhere in the area.

CFI completed trail construction and restoration work on Mount Harvard in 1999–2002.

**GETTING THERE:** From Buena Vista, turn west on Chaffee County Road 350 (Crossman Avenue), and drive for 2 miles, then turn north and drive for 1 mile. At the sign for North Cottonwood Creek, turn south and drive for 0.2 mile, then turn west and head west and northwest for 5 miles to the end of a passable road. Park here and backpack in.

**THE ROUTE:** After leaving the parking area, the trail crosses a bridge to the south side of the creek and proceeds westward 1.5 miles, to a trail junction just after the trail returns to the north side of the creek on a second bridge. Take the right-hand trail, marked Horn Fork Basin, northwest, then north 2.5 miles to timberline. Camp in this area.

From camp, follow the North Cottonwood Trail 1.25 miles to the basin below Mount Harvard. The trail veers right, up and across a talus field near Bear Lake. Continue north up the steep grass and rock ridge. Proceed under the crest of the south shoulder of the summit block, and scramble up large boulders to the summit.

The Colorado Fourteeners Initiative recommended nontechnical route to Columbia from Harvard is to descend southeast into the Frenchman Creek drainage and then back up Columbia's north slope about a half mile from the summit. Return the way you came. The western scree slopes of Columbia have been severely impacted and eroded by climbers (there is no constructed trail).

**HISTORY:** In 1869, Josiah Dwight Whitney, a graduate of Yale and a professor at Harvard, led the first class of the Harvard Mining School into the Sawatch Range to explore rumors of 17,000-foot peaks. They climbed and named Mounts Harvard and Yale. Roger W. Toll, later superintendent of Rocky Mountain National Park, named Mount Columbia in 1916 after his own alma mater.

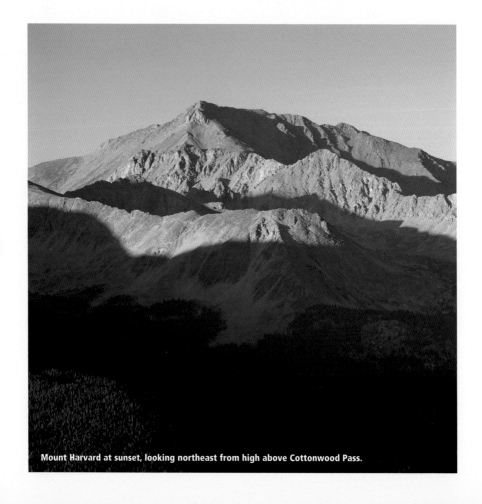

Mount Harvard at sunset, looking northeast from high above Cottonwood Pass.

Looking north down Ptarmigan Creek toward Mount Yale.

# Mount Yale

## 14,196 feet

| MAPS | Trails Illustrated 129–Buena Vista/Collegiate Peaks; Mount Yale 7.5 minute |
| --- | --- |
| RATING | More difficult |
| ELEVATION GAIN | 4,300 feet |
| ROUND-TRIP DISTANCE | 8 miles |
| ROUND-TRIP TIME | 8 hours |
| NEAREST TOWN | Buena Vista |
| RANGER DISTRICT | US Forest Service, Salida Ranger District, 719-539-3591 |

**COMMENT:** The old standard route up Mount Yale—the Denny Gulch Trail—has been closed. The new standard route is called the Denny Creek Trail.

Colorado Fourteeners Initiative and the US Forest Service have been working on trail construction on this route since 2008 and will continue through at least 2011. The route may change somewhat.

**GETTING THERE:** From Buena Vista, drive west on Chaffee County Road 306 along Middle Cottonwood Creek for 12 miles. Park near the Denny Creek Trailhead and sign the register (on the right side of the road).

**THE ROUTE:** You will be following a wide trail and will make two creek crossings. When you reach a fork, bear right and proceed northwest for 0.25 mile to an intersection that should be marked. Take the right fork into Delaney Gulch. Follow the trail to the south ridge and continue along the ridge to the summit. Descend the way you came.

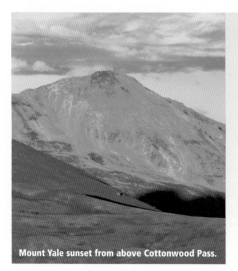

**Mount Yale sunset from above Cottonwood Pass.**

**HISTORY:** When Yale grads climbed and named Mount Yale in 1869, they initiated the Collegiate Peaks' naming tradition. The long-used southern approach via Denny Gulch is a good example of what overuse can do to a moderate route. In 1992, the Forest Service closed it, and now directs hikers to the summit via Denny Creek and Delaney Gulch.

**Cloud-to-ground lightning at 9,000 feet. You have been warned.**

## SIDEBAR: **A LIGHTNING PROTOCOL**

So you are caught in the middle of a thunderstorm and lightning is striking all around you, even below. You are remembering that the temperature of lightning is somewhat in excess of the temperature of the surface of the sun, that a fairly common lightning bolt can be 500 million volts, and that lightning often travels across wet ground.

What to do? Get off the ridge. FAST. Get off the trail, because there's a good chance that it's a gully that can conduct lightning. Stay away from rock overhangs. Once you are off the ridge, put your pack and rope on the ground as an insulator. Sit on top of your pack with your arms around your knees and your feet together, close your eyes, put your hands over your ears, and think good thoughts. Try to be invisible.

Mount Princeton from the northeast.

# Mount Princeton
## 14,197 feet

| MAPS | Trails Illustrated 130–Salida/St. Elmo/Mount Shavano; Mount Antero 7.5 minute |
|---|---|
| RATING | Moderate |
| ELEVATION GAIN | 3,200 feet |
| ROUND-TRIP DISTANCE | 6 miles |
| ROUND-TRIP TIME | 7 hours |
| NEAREST TOWN | Buena Vista |
| RANGER DISTRICT | US Forest Service, Salida Ranger District, 719-539-3591 |

**COMMENT:** On a hot summer day, you can go through a good deal of water on this route. Take extra. The standard route is the Mount Princeton Road Route up the southeast ridge.

**GETTING THERE:** From Buena Vista, drive south on US 285 for 8 miles, then turn west on County Road 162 to Chalk Creek Road. Turn right at Mount Princeton Hot Springs Inn. Continue up along the road through the Young Life Camp and follow the road as far as the TV relay station at 10,800 feet. How passable this road is depends on the vehicle and the season. There is a good campsite where the stream branches.

**THE ROUTE:** Hike along the road for about 1 to 1.5 miles beyond the TV relay station to where the road emerges from timber, just short of the boulder field. From this point, the A-frame Young Life chalet is visible. About 100 yards farther, a trail leaves the road uphill to the right. The trailhead is not obvious unless you go too far and look back. Follow this good trail until within 0.5 mile or less of the mine at its end. Cut left, up to a ridge that offers good access to the summit along a rocky, but usually dry, route.

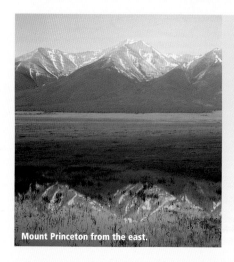

Mount Princeton from the east.

**HISTORY:** William Libbey, Jr., a professor of geology at Princeton, made the first recorded ascent of this peak on July 17, 1877. The proximity, however, of the Hortense mine at 12,000 feet, a rich silver producer, suggests an earlier ascent by miners. The Chalk Cliffs on the mountain's south side are actually crumbling white quartz monzonite.

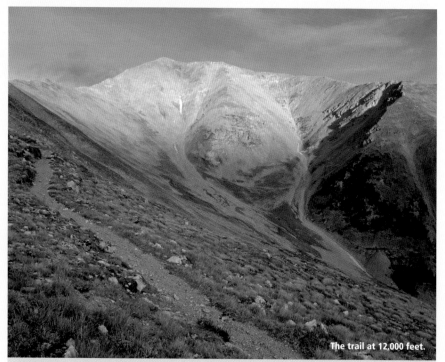

The trail at 12,000 feet.

## SIDEBAR: GEARING UP IN THE DARK

On one very long route, we saw a grad-student-looking fellow wearing two different shoes: a sloppy old leather shoe and a tennis shoe. When we asked him about the unique gear, he said he had camped the night before and put his shoes on in the dark and had not discovered his mistake until he was a mile or so from camp.

TRAILHEAD

Mount Princeton
(Elev 14197)

# Mount Antero
## 14,269 feet

| MAPS | Trails Illustrated 130–Salida/St. Elmo/Mount Shavano; Mount Antero 7.5 minute, St. Elmo 7.5 minute |
|------|-----------------------------------------------------------------|
| RATING | Moderate |
| ELEVATION GAIN | 3,300 feet |
| ROUND-TRIP DISTANCE | 8 miles |
| ROUND-TRIP TIME | 8 hours |
| NEAREST TOWN | Buena Vista |
| RANGER DISTRICT | US Forest Service, Salida Ranger District, 719-539-3591 |

**COMMENT:** Quartz, aquamarine, and topaz crystals are common in this area, and you may come across geologists and miners who have driven up to near the summit on the jeep road. This is not exactly your "one-with-the-mountain" climbing experience. It is more of a "four-wheel-drives-careening-downhill-get-the-right-of-way" sort of experience. The standard route is the Baldwin Gulch Route.

**GETTING THERE:** From Buena Vista, drive south on US 285 for 8 miles, then turn west on County Road 162 for 9.5 miles to Cascade Campground. Camp here, and in the morning, drive another 2 miles west on County Road 162 to Baldwin Gulch Road at 9,239 feet. Turn left (south) and follow rugged Baldwin Gulch Road for 3 miles to a creek crossing at about 11,000 feet and park. This road is for four-wheel-drives.

**THE ROUTE:** Hike across the creek and follow the road, which has a number of switchbacks up the broad slopes above you. At 13,100 feet, there is a shortcut to the left, or you may also stay on the road until just short of the summit. The final ascent is up a trail through talus.

Left. Looking northwest to Mount Antero from Mount White.

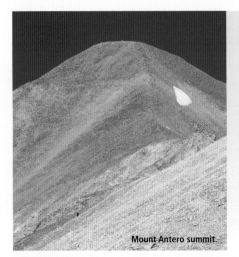

Mount Antero summit.

**HISTORY:** Antero was a prominent Ute chief who promoted peace with the incoming white settlers. Nathaniel Wanemaker discovered Mount Antero's famous blue aquamarine crystals in 1884. In recent years, good gem finds have decreased, but Mount Antero remains the highest mineral locality in North America.

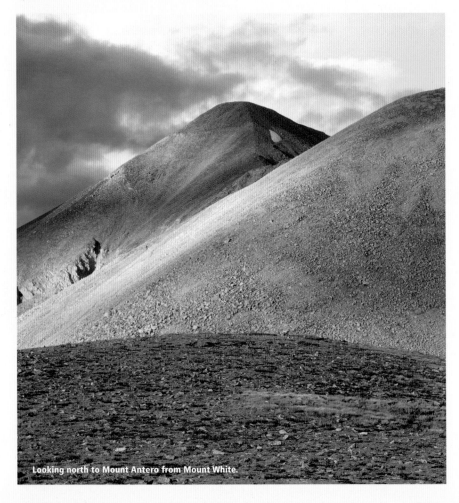

Looking north to Mount Antero from Mount White.

Mount Antero from the northeast.

Tabeguache Peak from the south.

# Mount Shavano 14,229 feet
# Tabeguache Peak 14,155 feet

| | |
|---|---|
| **MAPS** | Trails Illustrated 130–Salida/St. Elmo/Mount Shavano; St. Elmo 7.5 minute, Mount Antero 7.5 minute, Garfield 7.5 minute, Maysville 7.5 minute |
| **RATING** | Moderate |
| **ELEVATION GAIN** | 4,430 feet, plus you lose and regain 500 feet in the saddle in each direction |
| **ROUND-TRIP DISTANCE** | 9 miles |
| **ROUND-TRIP TIME** | 9 to 10 hours |
| **NEAREST TOWN** | Poncha Springs |
| **RANGER DISTRICT** | US Forest Service, Salida Ranger District, 719-539-3591 |

**COMMENT:** These two Fourteeners are usually climbed together. The US Forest Service and the Colorado Fourteeners Initiative recommend that Shavano be climbed first and Tabeguache (pronounced tab-a-wash) be climbed second. The Blank Gulch Route is the standard route.

The CFI strongly recommends against using the Jennings Creek approach to Tabeguache, as it is seriously eroded, unstable, and dangerous with very unstable, erosive soils. Climbers who use this route are undoing restoration work that has been done by CFI staff and volunteers.

**GETTING THERE:** Drive on US 50 west from Salida to Poncha Springs. Go through Poncha Springs and continue west on US 50 for an additional 2 miles to County Road 250. Turn north and follow County Road 250 for 4.8 miles, then bear left onto County Road 252 and continue for approximately another 3 miles to Mount Shavano/Tabeguache Peak Trailhead. The trailhead is at a stone monument that marks the old Blank Cabin. The monument honors L. Dale Hibbs, who promoted Rocky Mountain goat protection.

**THE ROUTE:** Walk northwest approximately 0.1 mile to an intersection with the Colorado Trail, then turn right and walk for 0.3 mile to the intersection with the Mount Shavano Trail. Turn west (left). From the Colorado Trail intersection to the saddle just south of Mount Shavano

131

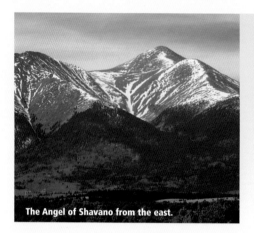

The Angel of Shavano from the east.

**HISTORY:** Mount Shavano, Tabeguache Peak, neighboring Mount Antero, and Uncompahgre Peak are the only four Four-teeners that bear names of Native American origin. Shavano was a prominent chief of the Tabeguache band of Utes. His name appears on the mountain on maps as early as 1875.

is 3.5 miles. From this point on, the trail is not clearly marked. Follow the ridge to the summit of Mount Shavano, approximately 0.5 mile ahead of you. From the summit of Shavano, descend northwest for 0.75 mile to the saddle at 13,700 feet, then climb 0.25 mile west to Tabeguache's summit. Return by the same route. Do not try to skirt Shavano's summit on the way back, since you may end up in McCoy Gulch and in trouble.

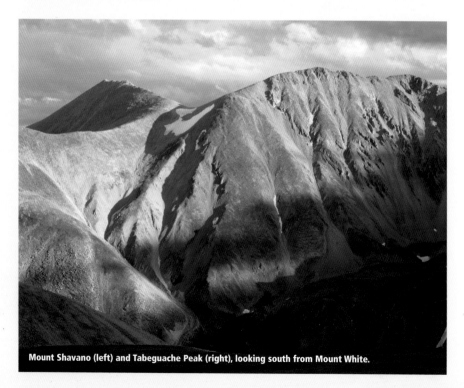

Mount Shavano (left) and Tabeguache Peak (right), looking south from Mount White.

# Capitol Peak
## 14,130 feet

| MAPS | Trails Illustrated 128–Maroon Bells/Redstone/Marble; Capitol Peak 7.5 minute |
|------|------|
| RATING | Very difficult |
| ELEVATION GAIN | 4,900 feet |
| ROUND-TRIP DISTANCE | 16 miles from the trailhead |
| ROUND-TRIP TIME | 16 hours |
| NEAREST TOWN | Aspen |
| RANGER DISTRICT | US Forest Service, Aspen Ranger District, 970-925-3445 |

**COMMENT:** Wear a climbing helmet and pack a rope. Watch the weather constantly. The ridge is exposed, and lightning storms are frequent from April to September. The standard route is the Capitol Lake Route and up the northeast ridge.

**GETTING THERE:** From Aspen, drive approximately 14 miles toward Glenwood Springs on Colorado 82 until you reach County Road 11 on the left. Turn left (south) and drive almost 2 miles. Keep right at the fork and continue less than 0.5 mile to the next fork. There, keep left. Continue 1.5 miles southwest to another fork. Take the right fork. Follow County Road 9 for approximately 4 miles, to an area where there are several cabins to the right of the road. Most passenger cars should be able to drive another 1.5 miles to a meadow at 9,400 feet.

**THE ROUTE:** The Capitol Creek Trail drops 400 feet to the left of the meadow, but a jeep road leaves the upper end of the meadow to Williams Lake and Hardscrabble Lake. At the point where the jeep road crosses a ditch on a bridge, there is a trail that follows the ditch to the left of the road. This trail joins the Capitol Creek Trail without the 400-foot loss in elevation, but you may encounter a problematic stream crossing, especially during runoff, before you can rejoin the trail.

Backpack south from the meadow for 6.5 miles along Capitol Creek Trail to the north end of Capitol Lake at 11,600 feet. Camp here. Follow all the Forest Service regulations when you camp, since camping rules are enforced vigorously in this area.

Left. Capitol Peak at sunset, as seen from the Capitol Creek Trailhead.

From the lake, the Capitol Creek Trail climbs east 0.5 mile to the Capitol-Daly ridge. Traverse several hundred feet on the east side of the ridge, then turn right and ascend to K2. Climb around the north side of K2 to reach the ridge before the knife-edge. After crossing the knife-edge, do an ascending traverse following cairns, to gain the northwest ridge. Follow the ridge to the summit.

**HISTORY:** Capitol Peak was named by the Hayden Survey for its resemblance to the US Capitol. Survey members made no attempt to climb it, because "its prism-shaped top and precipitous sides forbid access." This assessment held true until Percy Hagerman and Harold Clark reached the summit on August 22, 1909, via the knife-edged northeast ridge.

Capitol Peak from Silver Creek Pass.

## SIDEBAR: OH BUDDY, WE CAN MAKE IT

For reasons not worth discussing, we were late to the mountains, starting a two-mountain route at 10 a.m. The weather looked marginal. We almost trotted up the first peak, arriving exhausted and grumpy at noon. We dropped into the saddle between Belford and Oxford and were almost running toward the next peak. We were absolutely caught up in summit fever. There was only one problem: a thunderstorm was headed right at us.

The next peak was maybe a mile away at most. Some fool said the magic words, "Oh Buddy, we can make it." We went for the next peak and then beat feet back down into the saddle. The sky turned a gray-black. There was a moment of real silence and then a blast of wind at maybe forty knots screamed across the saddle. We were stopped in our tracks, huddled together. The wind came harder and harder, and then it went straight up, carrying snow pellets with it. We grabbed each other's pack harnesses to stay stable in the wind. And then the sky exploded like tons of explosives going off at once. We were on our knees, trying to survive. We were as scared as we had ever been. Instead of following *A Lightning Protocol* (page 120), we dropped off the ridge and started walking down. We split up so that if we took a lightning strike, it wouldn't kill both of us. One of us said to the other as we split up, "You jerk!"

Snowmass Mountain and Geneva Lake, looking north.

# Snowmass Mountain
## 14,092 feet

| MAPS | Trails Illustrated 128–Maroon Bells/Redstone/Marble; Snowmass Mountain 7.5 minute |
| --- | --- |
| RATING | More difficult or very difficult, depending on route |
| ELEVATION GAIN | 5,700 feet |
| ROUND-TRIP DISTANCE | 22 miles from the trailhead |
| ROUND-TRIP TIME | 18 hours |
| NEAREST TOWN | Aspen |
| RANGER DISTRICT | US Forest Service, Aspen Ranger District, 970-925-3445 |

**COMMENT:** The standard route is the Snowmass Lake Trail and up the southeast ridge.

**GETTING THERE:** From Aspen, drive approximately 14 miles toward Glenwood Springs on Colorado 82 until you reach County Road 11. Turn left (south) onto Snowmass Creek Road. After almost 2 miles, at a "T" junction, keep left and continue along Snowmass Creek Road to Snowmass Falls Ranch.

**THE ROUTE:** Backpack south 9 miles, gaining 2,600 feet in elevation, up Snowmass Creek to Snowmass Lake at 11,000 feet. Camp on the east side of the lake. From this approach the whole of Snowmass Mountain is in view to the right of Hagerman Peak. Hike 0.2 mile around the south shore of the lake and climb west into the basin, keeping to the right (north) of Hagerman Peak. Then, climb onto the ridge between Hagerman and Snowmass and follow the southeast ridge to the summit. This is a moderate, but long, ascent. The trail from Snowmass Lake to the plateau is extremely eroded and braided. Try to stay on the main trail and avoid creating new ones. When traveling off-trail, make sure to walk on durable surfaces like rock or snow. The tundra vegetation is extremely fragile and takes years to grow back.

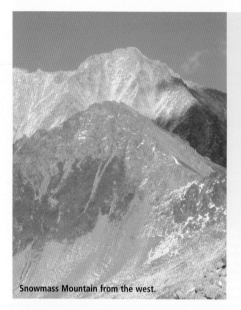

Snowmass Mountain from the west.

**HISTORY:** The inspiration for naming Snowmass is easy to understand when one surveys the perennial expanse of snow in the mountain's eastern cirque. Hayden Survey members made the first ascent in 1873 and resisted suggestions to call it "Whitehouse" to complement Capitol Peak. Bill Forest and Glen Denny first traversed the jagged, four-mile-long ridge between Snowmass and Capitol in 1966.

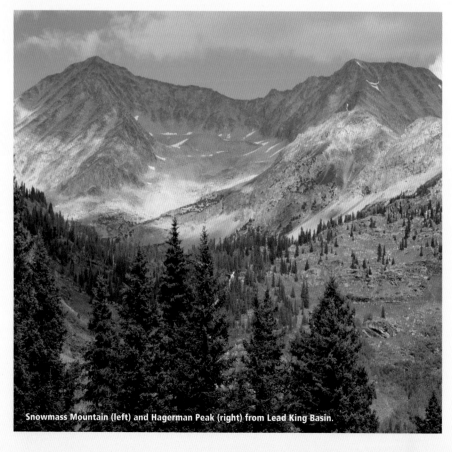

Snowmass Mountain (left) and Hagerman Peak (right) from Lead King Basin.

North Maroon Peak dominates the view from Crater Lake. Maroon Peak rises behind.

# North Maroon Peak

## 14,014 feet

| MAPS | Trails Illustrated 128–Maroon Bells/Redstone/Marble; Maroon Bells 7.5 minute |
|---|---|
| RATING | Very difficult |
| ELEVATION GAIN | 4,400 feet |
| ROUND-TRIP DISTANCE | 8 miles |
| ROUND-TRIP TIME | 11 hours |
| NEAREST TOWN | Aspen |
| RANGER DISTRICT | US Forest Service, Aspen Ranger District, 970-925-3445 |

**COMMENT:** See the comment for (South) Maroon Peak. The standard route is from the Maroon Lake Trailhead. The maximum drop between the twin summits is 234 feet across a difficult distance of 2,100 feet.

**GETTING THERE:** From Aspen, drive northwest 1.2 miles on Colorado 82 and turn left (south). Keep right at the fork that appears immediately on the road to Maroon Lake. Drive about 9 miles to the end of the road where there is a new designated parking lot for climbers. During the summer months, access to Maroon Lake has been restricted to buses from the parking lot.

**THE ROUTE:** From Maroon Lake, go 1.5 miles to a right fork that heads toward Buckskin Pass. Near timberline, drop west across a stream and go southwest 0.75 mile to a timberline bench. Head southeast to a rock glacier under the north face of North Maroon. Contour south around the east ridge into a wide couloir with rocky benches. Climb this couloir for about 0.3 mile to 12,600 feet. Exit the couloir on the left and turn a corner to ascend a second couloir. Eventually this couloir runs into the summit ridge at 13,200 feet. Cross through cliffs to reach the ridge crest and the north face. Proceed west to a chimney that can be climbed with a basic amount of technical knowledge. Climb west along the ridge to the summit.

Maroon and North Maroon peaks from Maroon Lake.

**HISTORY:** The Hayden and Wheeler surveys mapped and admired the Maroon Bells, which are named for their color and shape, but did not reach their summits. The Hayden team named the formation Maroon Mountain and regarded North Maroon as merely a sub-peak.

Maroon and North Maroon peaks with autumn aspens.

## SIDEBAR: POLYPRO

We wish we had a dollar for every person we have seen headed up Fourteener trails in cotton shorts and a T-shirt, carrying a bottle of water from the jiffy mart. Thousands of folks start that way, and many don't make it very far.

They aren't prepared for the route in a good number of ways, but their worst mistake is the cotton clothing. There is no describing just how cold they will feel in a wet cotton T-shirt with the wind blowing at 12,000 feet.

We're great fans of polypropylene T-shirts, shirts, vests, and jackets. Yes, you are right, polypro can get pretty skanky-smelling, but here are the advantages:

- Polypro will keep you warm even when it's wet. If you keep moving in wet polypro, you can stay fairly comfortable.
- Polypro dries very quickly. Take your shirt off and shake it in the wind a bit, and it will dry.
- Polypro wicks away sweat from your body.
- Polypro is lighter than wool and more compressible, for the same thickness of insulation.

TRAILHEAD

Telephoto view of Maroon Peak from Paradise Divide, looking northeast.

# (South) Maroon Peak
## 14,156 feet

| MAPS | Trails Illustrated 128–Maroon Bells/Redstone/Marble; Maroon Bells 7.5 minute |
|---|---|
| RATING | Very difficult |
| ELEVATION GAIN | 4,500 feet |
| ROUND-TRIP DISTANCE | 10 miles |
| ROUND-TRIP TIME | 12 hours |
| NEAREST TOWN | Aspen |
| RANGER DISTRICT | US Forest Service, Aspen Ranger District, 970-925-3445 |

**COMMENT:** The Maroon Bells and Pyramid Peak, which are among Colorado's most picturesque mountains, are also among the most dangerous. The primary hazards of loose and falling rock can be somewhat minimized by climbing in small parties and by going during the week, not on weekends. Wear a helmet and bring a rope. The standard route is from the Maroon Lake Trailhead and is called the South Ridge Route.

**GETTING THERE:** From Aspen, drive northwest 1.2 miles on Colorado 82 and turn left (south). Keep right at the fork that appears immediately on the road to Maroon Lake. Drive about 9 miles to the end of the road where there is a new designated parking lot for climbers. During the summer months, access to Maroon Lake has been restricted to buses from the parking lot.

**THE ROUTE:** From the north side of Maroon Lake, hike southwest to Crater Lake. Go around the western side of Crater Lake and head south for approximately 2 miles to what Gerry Roach and Louis Dawson call the South Ridge Route, which heads west to the ridgeline and then north to the summit. Much of the route is marked with cairns, but there are also a number of cairns that mislead climbers. If you feel you are off-route, backtrack.

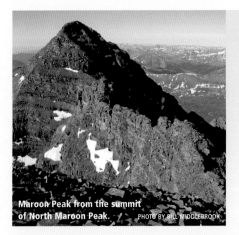

Maroon Peak from the summit of North Maroon Peak. PHOTO BY BILL MIDDLEBROOK

**HISTORY:** After their first ascent in 1908 by Percy Hagerman and Harold Clark, the Maroon Bells became a favorite destination for Colorado Mountain Club parties. On the 1940 Labor Day outing, the club had seventy-three people in base camp and forty people in the climbing party. Rock!

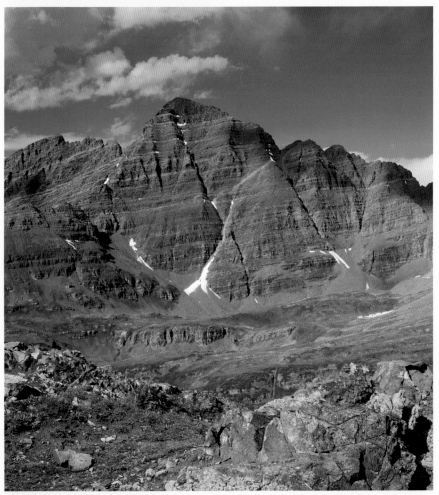

Maroon Peak viewed from Frigid Air Pass.

# Pyramid Peak
## 14,018 feet

| MAPS | Trails Illustrated 128–Maroon Bells/Redstone/Marble; Maroon Bells 7.5 minute |
| --- | --- |
| RATING | Very difficult |
| ELEVATION GAIN | 4,400 feet |
| ROUND-TRIP DISTANCE | 7 miles |
| ROUND-TRIP TIME | 10 hours |
| NEAREST TOWN | Aspen |
| RANGER DISTRICT | US Forest Service, Aspen Ranger District, 970-925-3445 |

**COMMENT:** See the comment for (South) Maroon Peak on page 147. The Northeast Ridge Route is standard.

CFI completed trail construction and restoration work leading from the valley to the base of the amphitheater in 2005–2006. A note about trails: When Fourteener trails are rerouted and constructed, it is primarily done to prevent and mitigate negative impacts to natural resources, particularly sensitive high-alpine vegetation. In locations like Pyramid Peak, when a trail reaches bedrock or boulders, trail construction stops, as there is no longer vegetation to be impacted. In these areas, you are responsible for route-finding.

**GETTING THERE:** From Aspen, drive northwest 1.2 miles on Colorado 82 and turn left (south). Keep right at the fork that appears immediately on the road to Maroon Lake. Drive about 9 miles to the end of the road where there is a new designated parking lot for climbers. During the summer months, access to Maroon Lake has been restricted to buses from the parking lot.

**THE ROUTE:** Take the trail past Maroon Lake toward Crater Lake. After about 1 mile, you will reach a rocky area marked with a large cairn to the left. Take the trail southeast across a moraine and climb steeply up the trail to the amphitheater. The Northeast Ridge Route climbs directly out of the basin to the lowest saddle on the east skyline. Then keep on the southeast side of the ridge and follow it to the summit.

Left. Pyramid Peak from the trail to Buckskin Pass.

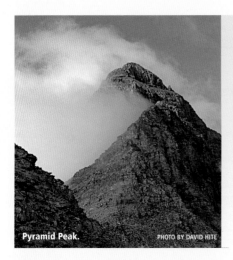

Pyramid Peak.    PHOTO BY DAVID HITE

**HISTORY:** The first documented ascent of Pyramid, a descriptive name bestowed by the surveys, came when Percy Hagerman and Harold Clark reached the summit on August 31, 1909. Hagerman had mining interests and Clark was a prominent Aspen attorney. Beginning in 1908, they climbed almost every major summit in the Elks.

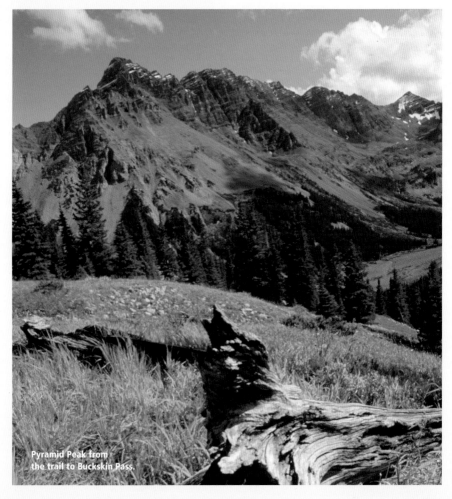

Pyramid Peak from the trail to Buckskin Pass.

Looking south toward Pyramid Peak from the Maroon Lake road.

# Castle Peak
## 14,265 feet

| MAPS | Trails Illustrated 127–Aspen/Independence Pass; Hayden Peak 7.5 minute |
|---|---|
| RATING | More difficult |
| ELEVATION GAIN | 4,400 feet from the trailhead |
| ROUND-TRIP DISTANCE | 13 miles from the trailhead |
| ROUND-TRIP TIME | 12 hours from the trailhead |
| NEAREST TOWN | Aspen |
| RANGER DISTRICT | US Forest Service, Aspen Ranger District, 970-925-3445 |

**COMMENT:** This peak is the highest, but also the least difficult to climb, in the Elk Range. The Montezuma Basin Route is standard.

**GETTING THERE:** From Aspen, drive northwest 1 mile on Colorado 82, then turn left (south) and take an immediate left-hand road to Ashcroft for 12 miles. Continue for 2 miles beyond Ashcroft. Turn right onto the smaller Pearl Pass Road, as the main road continues straight ahead and crosses Castle Creek. After another 0.5 mile, the road starts to climb at 9,900 feet. If using a conventional vehicle, park and camp in the aspen groves.

**THE ROUTE:** Either hike or use a four-wheel-drive vehicle to ascend about 2.5 miles to 11,000 feet, to the Pearl Pass Road junction, which is unmarked. Turn right and follow Montezuma Mine Road to the end, which is well over 12,000 feet. With a four-wheel-drive, this can be a very short route indeed.

One route is to climb from the end of the Montezuma Mine Road by heading southwest up the valley. At 13,400 feet, head south to gain the northeast ridge of Castle Peak. Follow the ridge to the summit. Descend by the same route, or descend the northwest ridge to the saddle between Castle Peak and Conundrum Peak. When snow is abundant, a long, exhilarating glissade is possible from the Conundrum saddle. See Lou Dawson's books for snow routes on the Fourteeners.

Left. Castle Peak with red indian paintbrush in the foreground, from the north side of Pearl Pass.

**HISTORY:** It is doubtful that Castle was climbed before 1873, when Henry Gannett led a Hayden Survey party up the difficult spires and pinnacles of its jagged south ridge. Gannett gave Castle Peak its descriptive name and reported that Castle "afforded more of a climb than any other Colorado mountain with which I have any acquaintance."

Castle Peak from the Conundrum-Castle saddle.   PHOTO BY BILL MIDDLEBROOK

Castle Peak.

San Luis Peak from the west.

# San Luis Peak

## 14,014 feet

| MAPS | Trails Illustrated 139–La Garita/Cochetopa Hills; San Luis Peak 7.5 minute, Stewart Peak 7.5 minute |
| --- | --- |
| RATING | Moderate |
| ELEVATION GAIN | 3,600 feet from the Stewart Creek Trailhead |
| ROUND-TRIP DISTANCE | 14 miles from the Stewart Creek Trailhead |
| ROUND-TRIP TIME | 14 hours from the Stewart Creek Trailhead |
| NEAREST TOWN | Gunnison |
| RANGER DISTRICT | US Forest Service, Gunnison Ranger District, 970-641-0471 |

**COMMENT:** The biggest challenge of climbing this peak is locating the Stewart Creek Trailhead to start the standard route.

CFI and the US Forest Service are planning trail construction and maintenance work for this route.

**GETTING THERE:** Coming from the north, take US 50 to the junction of Colorado 114 just east of Gunnison. It is approximately 47 miles to the trailhead from this intersection. Turn south onto Colorado 114. Drive about 20 miles and turn right onto the NN-14 road. Drive 6.7 miles to Dome Lakes and turn right onto the 15-GG dirt road (also known as FR 794 when you reach the National Forest). The road briefly goes around the lake where there is a small junction. Stay left on the main road. From the start of the 15-GG road, drive 15.7 miles to an intersection where there are signs. Follow the sign for the Stewart Creek Trailhead by continuing straight on the 794 road. Drive 4.2 miles to the trailhead. Be alert for the signed trailhead. Take a sharp right down into the small parking area.

**THE ROUTE:** Hike west up Stewart Creek Valley, keeping to the right (north) side of the creek most of the time. The trail is easily discernable. At the end of the valley you will see a high, flattened, pyramid-shaped peak. After climbing past several gulches coming in from the left, ascend to the saddle on the northwest slope of San Luis Peak. From this point, the summit can be seen 0.2 mile away in a west-southwest direction, but this is still a long hike.

**ALTERNATE ROUTE:** The Willow Creek Route starts at the end of the road at the Equity Mine. Head north about 3 miles to the intersection with the Continental Divide Trail (CDT). Go generally east on the CDT, and at about 12,600 feet, follow the CDT north. When the CDT heads to the northeast, break off to the northwest and continue up the south ridge of San Luis Peak to the summit.

**HISTORY:** San Luis Peak in the La Garita Mountains on the western edge of the San Luis Valley borrowed its name from the valley below. No record exists of its first ascent, but Utes probably were the first to reach its summit. The Los Pinos Agency for the Tabeguache Utes was located on Cochetopa Creek northeast of the peak.

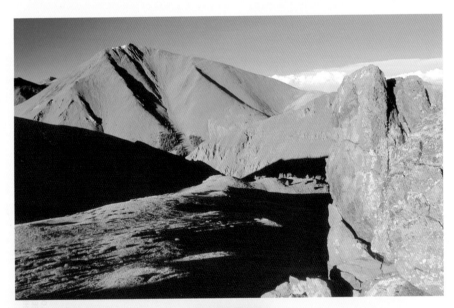

Top.
San Luis Peak, looking east from the Colorado Trail.

Left.
San Luis Peak, looking southwest from the Organ Mountain–San Luis Peak saddle.

Uncompahgre Peak, looking east from the slopes of Matterhorn Peak.

# Uncompahgre Peak
## 14,309 feet

| MAPS | Trails Illustrated 141–Telluride/Silverton/Ouray/Lake City; Uncompahgre Peak 7.5 minute |
| --- | --- |
| RATING | More difficult |
| ELEVATION GAIN | 3,900 feet |
| ROUND-TRIP DISTANCE | 11 miles |
| ROUND-TRIP TIME | 9 hours |
| NEAREST TOWN | Lake City |
| RANGER DISTRICT | US Forest Service, Gunnison Ranger District, 970-641-0471 |

**COMMENT:** Uncompahgre and Wetterhorn are sometimes climbed in one day; however, the Nellie Creek Route is strongly recommended. If climbing Uncompahgre from Matterhorn Basin, it is important to stay on the established trail all the way to the summit, due to the sensitivity of the alpine environment on Uncompahgre. The Nellie Creek Route is standard.

CFI has been working on heavy trail maintenance of this route in 2007–2009. A note about braided trails: Oftentimes, when hikers come across eroded trails, they walk next to the trail in search of a more stable and comfortable hiking surface. Unfortunately, as in the case of the trail leading up the Nellie Creek Valley at Uncompahgre Peak, this causes increasingly widened and braided trails (where multiple impacted trails run side by side). Practice Leave No Trace by always choosing to hike on the most impacted/eroded trail when you come across multiple parallel trails.

**GETTING THERE:** In Lake City, find County Road 20 and drive west for about 5 miles. Turn north (right) onto the Nellie Creek Road. This road is not recommended for a passenger car. The road has steep switchbacks and can be slippery during wet weather. A four-wheel-drive vehicle is advisable. Park at the end of the road.

**THE ROUTE:** The Nellie Creek Trail is well traveled and easy to follow. It goes west to the southeast ridge of Uncompahgre, and then north up to the summit.

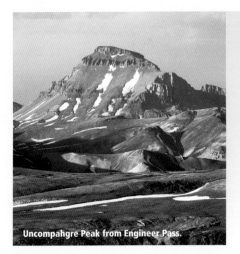

Uncompahgre Peak from Engineer Pass.

**HISTORY:** Uncompahgre was probably first climbed by Utes. The name is a Ute word said to mean "hot water spring." The Hayden Survey named the mountain after the Uncompahgre River. A. D. Wilson and Franklin Rhoda made the first documented ascent in 1874, and found that grizzly bears had preceded them to the summit.

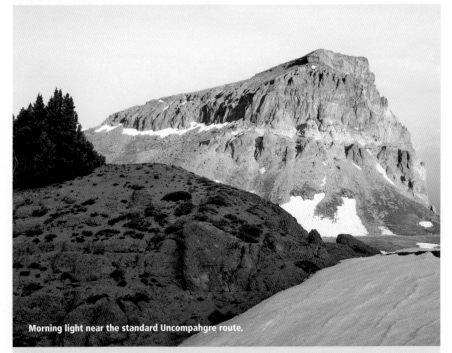

Morning light near the standard Uncompahgre route.

## SIDEBAR: THE REST STEP

There are a number of theories about the most efficient way to hike a Fourteener. Here's what works for us. It's an old mountaineering trick called the "Rest Step," where you move one foot upward, pause, take a breath, move your other foot up next to the uphill foot, pause, take a breath, then move that foot uphill and pause, and take a breath. It's slow, but when your lungs are screaming for oxygen, it works.

Wetterhorn Peak, looking southeast from West Fork Pass.

# Wetterhorn Peak
## 14,015 feet

| MAPS | Trails Illustrated 141–Telluride/Silverton/Ouray/Lake City; Wetterhorn Peak 7.5 minute |
| --- | --- |
| RATING | More difficult |
| ELEVATION GAIN | 3,600 feet |
| ROUND-TRIP DISTANCE | 8 miles |
| ROUND-TRIP TIME | 7 hours |
| NEAREST TOWN | Lake City |
| RANGER DISTRICT | US Forest Service, Gunnison Ranger District, 970-641-0471 |

**COMMENT:** There is a memorable final pitch on Wetterhorn, and all those black marks on the summit rocks are probably from lightning strikes. The Matterhorn Creek Route is standard.

CFI completed trail construction and restoration work in 2004.

**GETTING THERE:** From Lake City, go west on Henson Creek Road. Start measuring mileage from here. At 8.8 miles, there is a junction. Turn right and follow the sign for North Henson Road. At 10.8 miles, there is another junction with a sign that indicates the Matterhorn Creek trailhead is ahead. Park here if you don't have a high-clearance four-wheel-drive vehicle or turn right and continue on a rough four-wheel-drive road to the trailhead and parking area at 11.4 miles.

**THE ROUTE:** Hike north along the Ridgestock Driveway to the junction with the Wetterhorn Peak Trail. This junction is marked with a sign. Follow the established trail across Matterhorn Basin to the southeast summit ridgeline. Work up the ridgeline to the summit on a system of ledges. The route appears to be steep and formidable, but it goes well if the route is dry.

**WETTERHORN AND UMCOMPAHGRE TOGETHER:** If climbing Uncompahgre from Matterhorn Basin, it is important to stay on the established trail all the way to the summit, due to the sensitivity of the alpine environment on Uncompahgre. This is a very long climb.

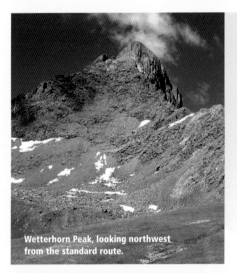

Wetterhorn Peak, looking northwest from the standard route.

**HISTORY:** Wetterhorn was named by Lieutenant William Marshall during the 1874 Wheeler Survey. Viewing it from nearby Uncompahgre, Marshall wrote, "The Wetterhorn ... is a shark's nose ... and appears inaccessible." Apparently, Marshall was familiar with the Wetterhorn in the Swiss Alps, to which he likened the Colorado peak.

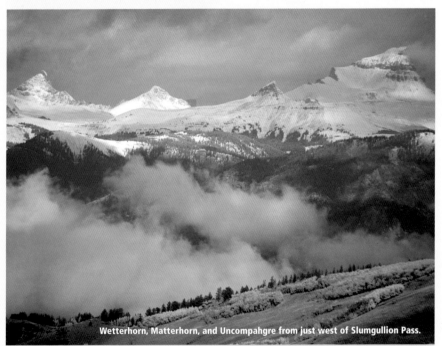

Wetterhorn, Matterhorn, and Uncompahgre from just west of Slumgullion Pass.

## SIDEBAR: WATER

We got lost and spent hours in an endless talus field on a hot day. We climbed a false summit. We ran out of water on the real summit. We were very dry when we got to the car. Carry more water than you think you will need. You have been warned.

Sunshine Peak from Cinnamon Pass, looking east at sunset.

# Redcloud Peak 14,034 feet
# Sunshine Peak 14,001 feet

| | |
|---|---|
| MAPS | Trails Illustrated 141–Telluride/Silverton/Ouray/Lake City; Redcloud Peak 7.5 minute |
| RATING | More difficult |
| ELEVATION GAIN | 3,600 feet, plus you lose and regain 500 feet in the saddle in each direction |
| ROUND-TRIP DISTANCE | 11 miles |
| ROUND-TRIP TIME | 10 hours |
| NEAREST TOWN | Lake City |
| RANGER DISTRICT | Bureau of Land Management, Gunnison Resource Area, 970-641-0471 |

**COMMENT:** Redcloud and Sunshine are traditionally done together. The Silver Creek Route is the standard route. Multiple braided trails exist between Redcloud and Sunshine peaks. Try to hike on the most prominent of these trails to prevent further impacts.

**GETTING THERE:** From Lake City, drive approximately 15 miles up the Lake Fork of the Gunnison River on County Road 30. Take the right fork onto County Road 4 toward Cinnamon Pass and drive for just over 4 miles to Grizzly Creek at 10,400 feet. There is an excellent campsite near Grizzly Gulch in the area of Silver Creek with water (not potable) and an outhouse.

**THE ROUTE:** Using the standard cairn route, hike northeast up the trail 2 miles to the northwest side of Silver Creek. Continue on the trail along the creek. At timberline, cross the creek, gain the saddle northeast of Redcloud, and climb the ridge southwest for 1 mile to the summit of Redcloud.

To get to Sunshine, follow the Redcloud ridge south for 1.5 miles. You will drop 500 feet between peaks. Return over Redcloud. In the saddle between Redcloud and Sunshine there is an apparent "descent" into the South Fork drainage that looks very inviting. It is steep, dangerous, and contains tricky talus. Once you take this wrong trail, it is extremely difficult to retrace your steps back to the saddle to access the safer route.

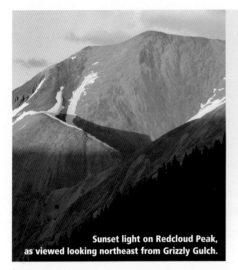

**Sunset light on Redcloud Peak, as viewed looking northeast from Grizzly Gulch.**

**HISTORY:** A palette of reds, yellows, and oranges dots Redcloud's rounded slopes, and it was informally called Red Mountain. J. C. Spiller of the Wheeler Survey upgraded this name to the poetic Redcloud in 1874. Later that summer, Hayden Survey members were chased off neighboring Sunshine Peak by lightning.

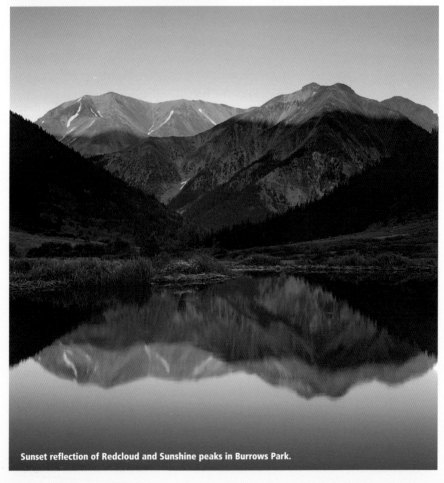

**Sunset reflection of Redcloud and Sunshine peaks in Burrows Park.**

Redcloud Peak from high in Grizzly Gulch.

TRAILHEAD

Handies Peak's reflection, looking southeast.

# Handies Peak

## 14,048 feet

| MAPS | Trails Illustrated 141–Telluride/Silverton/Ouray/Lake City; Handies Peak 7.5 minute, Redcloud 7.5 minute |
| --- | --- |
| RATING | Moderate |
| ELEVATION GAIN | 3,600 feet for the Grizzly Gulch Route |
| ROUND-TRIP DISTANCE | 8 miles for the Grizzly Gulch Route |
| ROUND-TRIP TIME | 6 hours for the Grizzly Gulch Route |
| NEAREST TOWN | Lake City |
| RANGER DISTRICT | Bureau of Land Management, Gunnison Resource Area, 970-641-0471 |

**COMMENT:** There are two standard routes, the American Basin Route and the Grizzly Gulch Route.

**GETTING THERE:** From Lake City, drive approximately 15 miles up the Lake Fork of the Gunnison River on County Road 30. Take the right fork onto County Road 4 toward Cinnamon Pass and drive for just over 4 miles to Grizzly Creek at 10,400 feet. There is an excellent campsite near Grizzly Gulch in the area of Silver Creek with water (not potable) and an outhouse.

**THE ROUTE:** Cross the Lake Fork of the Gunnison River, and hike up the Grizzly Gulch Trail out of the valley and west to the ridge. From the ridge it is an easy climb south to the summit.

**ALTERNATE ROUTE:** An easier 4- to 5-hour round-trip climb, that has an elevation gain of only 2,700 feet, is possible from the American Basin. Continue south on Cinnamon Pass Road for about 3.5 miles past Grizzly Creek. Take a four-wheel-drive road heading south into American Basin. Park along this road. Follow the road as it changes into a trail and begins to climb up grassy slopes. Continue south, then east to the south ridge of Handies, then north to the summit. Return by the same route, following the trail.

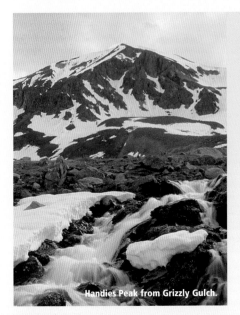

Handies Peak from Grizzly Gulch.

**HISTORY:** Despite the beauty and rich mining history surrounding this mountain, little is known of its name or first ascent. Miners likely account for both. Prominent nearby silver mines included the Bonhomme, Champion, Cracker Jack, and Tabasco, the latter on the road to Cinnamon Pass and financed by the Tabasco Meat Sauce Company. In fact, Handies was sometimes referred to as "Tabasco."

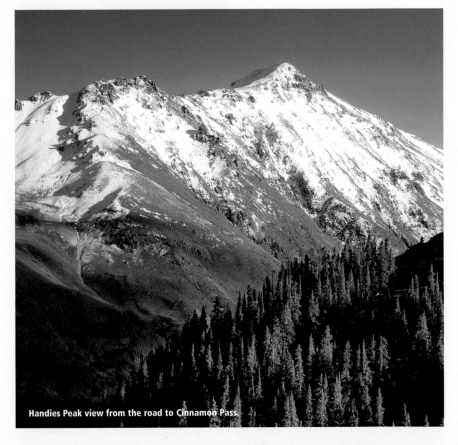

Handies Peak view from the road to Cinnamon Pass.

# Sunlight Peak 14,059 feet
# Windom Peak 14,082 feet

| MAPS | Trails Illustrated 140–Weminuche Wilderness; Mountain View Crest 7.5 minute, Columbine Pass 7.5 minute, Storm King Peak 7.5 minute |
| --- | --- |
| RATING | Very difficult |
| ELEVATION GAIN | 2,600 feet from camp, plus you lose and regain 1,000 feet between Sunlight and Windom |
| ROUND-TRIP DISTANCE | 5 miles from camp |
| ROUND-TRIP TIME | 5 hours from camp |
| NEAREST TOWN | Durango |
| RANGER DISTRICT | US Forest Service, Columbine Ranger District, 970-884-2512 |

COMMENT: Windom and Sunlight are close together, with 1,000 feet of elevation loss on the route connecting them. They should be climbed on the same day, unless weather dictates otherwise. Mount Eolus can also be climbed from the same high camp. Carrying a rope is a good idea. The Chicago Basin Route is standard, with a return to the flats and back up Windom to the east.

CFI has done trail construction work from the base of Chicago Basin leading to Twin Lakes, to continue from Twin Lakes toward Sunlight and Windom peaks in 2010 and beyond. Please stay on existing trails, and do not cause further impacts by hiking off-trail. Due to high levels of camping use and irresponsible behavior by some campers, Chicago Basin has a high level of impact (exposed human feces and campsites that are too close to water). To minimize impacts of your visit, always follow the following Leave-No-Trace rules: 1) Camp in established/impacted sites instead of forming new ones; 2) Camp below tree line to avoid impacts to sensitive alpine vegetation; 3) Camp at least 200 feet away from water; and 4) Bury human waste 6–8 inches deep and at least 200 feet away from water and campsites … or better yet, pack it out in sanitary bags (human waste bags are available at most outdoor retailer stores).

Left. Sunlight Peak, looking west from high in Sunlight Basin.

**GETTING THERE:** To reach the trailhead, take the Durango and Silverton Railroad from Durango. Call early for reservations: 970-247-2733. When you disembark at Needleton, cross the river on the suspension bridge and backpack east 7.2 miles up the trail along Needle Creek. Camp in Chicago Basin at about 11,000 feet, in the area where the trail crosses to the south bank of Needle Creek and starts up Columbine Pass.

**HISTORY:** Windom was named for William Windom, a senator from Minnesota and secretary of the treasury in 1881. When Hayden Survey topographer Franklin Rhoda viewed the Needle Mountains from a distance in 1874, he wrote that the range always gave his companions a feeling of uneasiness when they observed the frequent storm clouds hovering around the pointy summits.

**THE ROUTE:** Follow Needle Creek and the good trail north 1 mile to Twin Lakes at 12,500 feet. Turn east up the large basin between Sunlight and Windom. Keep to the left of Peak 18 (13,472 feet), the dominant feature on the ascent. Continue east 0.2 mile and climb southeast to the west ridge of Windom at 13,250 feet, near the Peak 18–Windom Peak col, a depression in the crest of the ridge. Continue east along the ridge for 0.2 mile to the summit. Descend 1,000 feet back down to the flatlands via the ascent route, and then head northeast to pass near the saddle between Sunlight Peak and a sub-peak to its southeast. Head northwest to the summit, and descend via the same route.

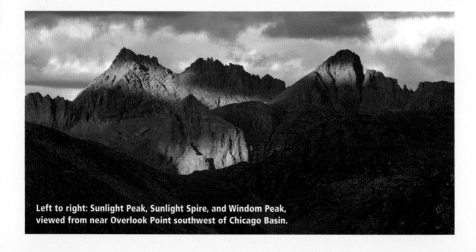

Left to right: Sunlight Peak, Sunlight Spire, and Windom Peak, viewed from near Overlook Point southwest of Chicago Basin.

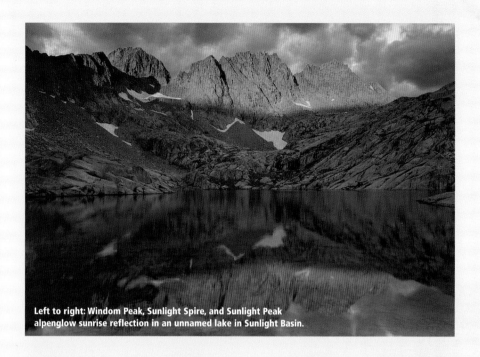

Left to right: Windom Peak, Sunlight Spire, and Sunlight Peak alpenglow sunrise reflection in an unnamed lake in Sunlight Basin.

Sunset on Mount Eolus, looking north from near Overlook Point.

# Mount Eolus
## 14,083 feet

| MAPS | Trails Illustrated 140–Weminuche Wilderness; Mountain View Crest 7.5 minute, Columbine Pass 7.5 minute, Storm King Peak 7.5 minute |
| --- | --- |
| RATING | Very difficult |
| ELEVATION GAIN | 2,800 feet from camp |
| ROUND-TRIP DISTANCE | 4 miles from camp |
| ROUND-TRIP TIME | 6 hours from camp |
| NEAREST TOWN | Durango |
| RANGER DISTRICT | US Forest Service, Columbine Ranger District, 970-884-2512 |

**COMMENT:** Mount Eolus can be climbed from the same Chicago Basin high camp that you use for Windom and Sunlight. The Chicago Basin Route is standard.

CFI is planning trail construction work on this route.

**GETTING THERE:** To reach the trailhead, take the Durango and Silverton Railroad from Durango. Call early for reservations: 970-247-2733. When you disembark at Needleton, cross the river on the suspension bridge and backpack east 7.2 miles up the trail along Needle Creek. Camp in Chicago Basin at about 11,000 feet, in the area where the trail crosses to the south bank of Needle Creek and starts up Columbine Pass.

**THE ROUTE:** From Chicago Basin, follow the trail north toward Twin Lakes. Before you get to Twin Lakes, head west. As you approach the great east face of Eolus, head northeast up a slab to the saddle between Eolus and Glacier Point at 13,700 feet. Turn west-southwest to the saddle between Eolus and North Eolus. Traverse southwest across a narrow and exposed ridge that enjoys the names "Sidewalk in the Sky" and "Catwalk." The ridge terminates in the east face of Eolus. Use the ledges on the face, keeping to the left and taking care to select the route to ascend to the summit.

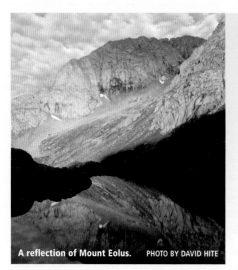

**A reflection of Mount Eolus.**     PHOTO BY DAVID HITE

**HISTORY:** Franklin Rhoda's assessment during the Hayden Survey that the Needle Mountains were a "regular manufactory of storms" inspired naming the highest peak there after Aeolus, the Greek god of the winds. Prospectors soon entered the area and staked claims in Chicago Basin, most likely scaling Mount Eolus and neighboring peaks.

Mount Eolus from North Eolus.     PHOTO BY DAVID HITE

Mount Eolus (left) and North Eolus from the east.

# Mount Sneffels
## 14,150 feet

| MAPS | Trails Illustrated 141–Telluride/Silverton/Ouray/Lake City; Mount Sneffels 7.5 minute, Telluride 7.5 minute |
|---|---|
| RATING | More difficult |
| ELEVATION GAIN | 2,400 feet |
| ROUND-TRIP DISTANCE | 2 miles |
| ROUND-TRIP TIME | 3 to 4 hours |
| NEAREST TOWN | Ouray |
| RANGER DISTRICT | US Forest Service, Ouray Ranger District, 970-240-5300 |

**COMMENT:** A truly imposing mountain. The Yankee Boy Basin up toward Blue Lake Pass and then north is the standard route.

**GETTING THERE:** From US 550, 0.5 mile south of Ouray, turn right and drive 6.5 miles. The Yankee Boy Basin Road bears to the right all the way to its end. Drive to timberline and park. The Yankee Boy Basin Route is standard.

**THE ROUTE:** Follow the Yankee Boy Basin Road up Yankee Boy Basin—famous for its alpine wildflowers and hummingbirds—to its end, then pick up the Blue Lake Pass Trail. Follow this trail to 12,600 feet, then head northeast on the trail to gain a wide couloir. The couloir leads to a saddle at 13,500 feet. Turn northwest on the saddle and enter a narrower and steeper rock-filled couloir that leads up to the wall under the summit. Before reaching the end of this couloir, look for another much smaller and shorter couloir, and take it. It leads to the left and terminates in a V-shaped notch through which you can climb out onto the approach to the summit, about 100 yards above.

If either of these couloirs become too difficult because of snow, it may be possible to move to the west and approach the summit across the southwest face of Sneffels.

Left. Mount Sneffels from the north.

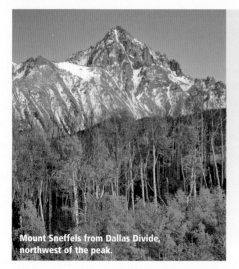

Mount Sneffels from Dallas Divide, northwest of the peak.

**HISTORY:** By most accounts, this mountain's name stems from the Hayden party's view of the peak rising above Blue Lakes Basin. Someone compared it to a dramatic scene from Jules Verne's *Journey to the Center of the Earth* and another exclaimed, "There's Snaefell!" A few insist it is from the "sniffles" suffered by many a high-altitude miner.

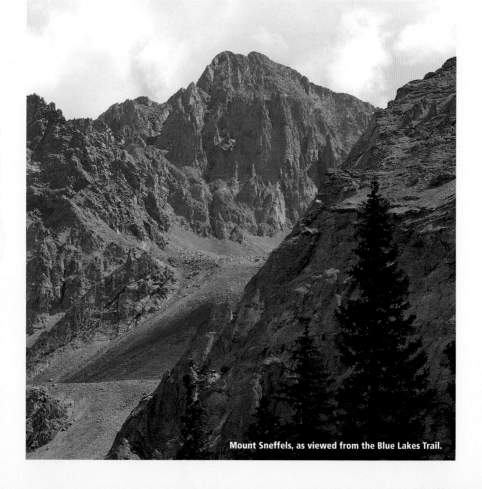

Mount Sneffels, as viewed from the Blue Lakes Trail.

Mount Sneffels, looking northwest from Black Bear Pass.

Wilson Peak from Wilson Mesa.

# Wilson Peak
## 14,017 feet

| MAPS | Trails Illustrated 141–Telluride/Silverton/Ouray/Lake City; Little Cone 7.5 minute, Gray Head 7.5 minute, Delores Peak 7.5 minute, Mount Wilson 7.5 minute |
|---|---|
| RATING | Very difficult |
| ELEVATION GAIN | 3,700 feet from the Rock of Ages Trailhead |
| ROUND-TRIP DISTANCE | 10 miles from the Rock of Ages Trailhead |
| ROUND-TRIP TIME | 12 hours from the Rock of Ages Trailhead |
| NEAREST TOWN | Placerville |
| RANGER DISTRICT | US Forest Service, Norwood Ranger District, 970-327-4261 |

**COMMENT:** The Colorado office of the Trust for Public Land purchased 230 acres in the Silver Pick Basin to help reestablish access to Wilson Peak via its standard southwest ridge route; also to Mount Wilson and El Diente via Rock of Ages saddle. Partners in this project estimate that public access to Silver Pick Basin via the Rock of Ages Trail will happen sometime in 2010 after this guide is published. The Telluride Mountain Club has been active in trail restoration on Wilson Peak. For access information, please contact either the Norwood District of the US Forest Service or The Colorado Mountain Club (303-279-3080) for current information.

**GETTING THERE:** From Placerville, drive 7 miles southeast to Vanadium on Colorado 145. Turn right up Big Bear Creek. At 4 miles south of Vanadium, take the center choice of three roads that is FR 622. Continuing south, at about 5.6 miles, bear off to the right. At 6.3 miles, bear off to the right again on FR 645 and find the trailhead at 8.5 miles.

**THE ROUTE:** Follow the trail from the Silver Pick Mine as it meanders south and up switchbacks to the saddle called "Rock of Ages." From the saddle, head east and then northeast to the summit.

**ALTERNATE ROUTE:** See the map for an alternate route from Navajo Basin. To get to Navajo Basin, follow the directions provided in the Mount Wilson section.

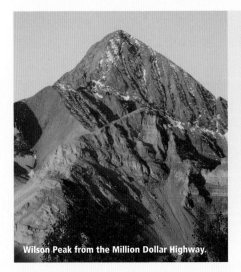

Wilson Peak from the Million Dollar Highway.

**HISTORY:** Wilson Peak and its higher neighbor, Mount Wilson, were both named for A. D. Wilson, the chief topographer for the Hayden Survey, which was responsible for exploring and mapping much of the Colorado Rockies in the 1870s. Mining remains dot the peak, including the Silver Pick Mine, the largest on the mountain.

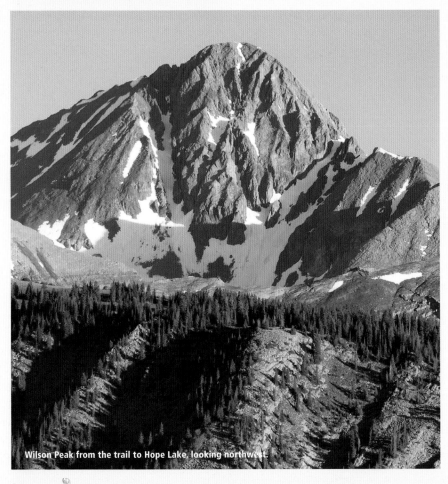

Wilson Peak from the trail to Hope Lake, looking northwest.

Springtime view of Wilson Peak from Silver Pick Road.

Rime ice-encrusted Mount Wilson, looking northwest from near Lizard Head Pass.

# Mount Wilson
## 14,246 feet

| MAPS | Trails Illustrated 141–Telluride/Silverton/Ouray/Lake City; Gray Head 7.5 minute, Delores Peak 7.5 minute |
| --- | --- |
| RATING | Very difficult |
| ELEVATION GAIN | 5,200 feet |
| ROUND-TRIP DISTANCE | 15 miles |
| ROUND-TRIP TIME | 15 hours |
| NEAREST TOWN | Telluride and Rico |
| RANGER DISTRICT | US Forest Service, Mancos-Dolores Ranger District, 970-882-7296 |

**COMMENT:** A climbing helmet and rope are advisable for this route, and bring an ice axe early in the season. Using the Kilpacker Creek approach (see the El Diente Peak section for directions), Mount Wilson and El Diente can be done in the same day by a strong party. As of the fall of 2009, the standard route is Navajo Basin, although the Silver Pick Basin Route, that is considerably shorter, may open in 2010.

**GETTING THERE:** To approach Mount Wilson through Navajo Basin, from just north of Telluride, drive south on Colorado 145 for 5.5 miles beyond Lizard Head Pass. Turn right (west) on Dunton Road (Forest Road 535). Follow Dunton Road for 6 miles, past Morgan Camp, to Forest Road 207. Then turn right for 0.2 mile on a short road that terminates in a parking area at West Dolores River. The Navajo Lake Trailhead is located at the northern end of the parking area. Follow the trail north along the river for 5 miles to Navajo Lake, where there are campsites east of the lake. Note that campfires are prohibited in the entire Navajo Basin.

**THE ROUTE:** Climb east to the head of Navajo Basin. At 12,300 feet, turn south and follow the ridge on the western side between Gladstone and Mount Wilson. This should enable you to skirt the permanent snowfield along the way. At 13,800 feet, head southwest to gain the northeast ridge of Mount Wilson. At 14,100 feet, head south through a notch in the ridge. This leads to a dramatic, exposed ridge that culminates in the summit. Descend using the same route.

Mount Wilson from Wilson Peak.
PHOTO BY BILL MIDDLEBROOK

**HISTORY:** A Hayden Survey party that included A. D. Wilson and Franklin Rhoda reached the summit of Mount Wilson via the difficult south ridge on September 13, 1874. Earlier that summer, J. C. Spiller of the Wheeler Survey had tried the route and failed. Mount Wilson remains a challenging climb from any direction.

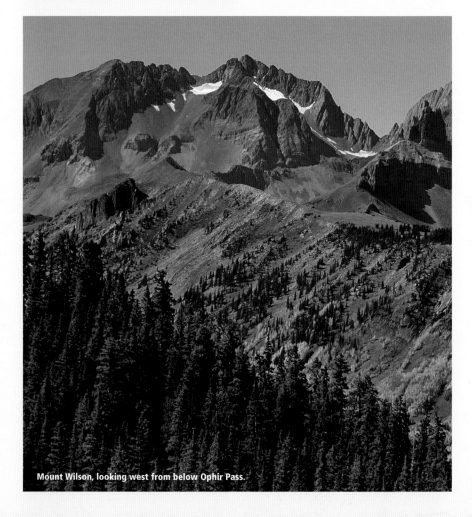

Mount Wilson, looking west from below Ophir Pass.

Sunrise on Mount Wilson, as viewed from the Hope Lake Trail.

El Diente Peak from Kilpacker Creek.

# El Diente Peak
## 14,159 feet

| MAPS | Trails Illustrated 141–Telluride/Silverton/Ouray/Lake City; Delores Peak 7.5 minute, Mount Wilson 7.5 minute |
|---|---|
| RATING | Very difficult |
| ELEVATION GAIN | 4,100 feet |
| ROUND-TRIP DISTANCE | 13 miles |
| ROUND-TRIP TIME | 12 hours |
| NEAREST TOWN | Telluride and Rico |
| RANGER DISTRICT | US Forest Service, Mancos-Dolores Ranger District, 970-882-7296 |

**COMMENT:** This is a difficult, dangerous, and challenging climb. It is strongly advised that you consult more detailed guides and carry the appropriate maps and equipment. A climbing helmet and rope are advisable for this route, and bring an ice axe early in the season. The standard route is the Silver Pick Basin Route, which is currently closed, but which may open in 2010. For this edition, the standard route is through Kilpacker Basin.

**GETTING THERE:** From Telluride, drive south on Colorado 145 for 5.5 miles beyond Lizard Head Pass. Turn right (west) on Dunton Road (Forest Road 535). After about 5.5 miles, as Dunton Road begins to lose altitude, turn right onto a small road that passes through a meadow. Continue for another 0.25 mile to a grove of trees where there is limited parking.

**THE ROUTE:** Hike on a closed jeep road northwest and then north and then northeast for 1.5 miles to Kilpacker Creek. Do not cross the creek. Just south of the creek, pick up a trail heading east and continue generally up along the creek after the trail crosses the creek and ends. Pass two waterfalls near timberline. Continue up the drainage to gain the Mount Wilson–El Diente ridge. Gain the ridge to the left, or west, of a formation called Organ Pipes. This route eliminates a difficult traverse around the formation. As you head for the summit, switch to the north side of the ridge.

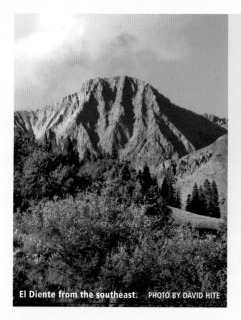

El Diente from the southeast.   PHOTO BY DAVID HITE

**HISTORY:** In 1930, Dwight Lavender, Forrest Greenfield, and Chester Price climbed the west ridge of what was then thought to be only the western sub-peak of Mount Wilson. Finding no evidence of a prior ascent, they claimed a first ascent and named it El Diente, Spanish for "the tooth." Later, Lavender discovered an ascent of Mount Wilson in August 1890 that he felt was in fact the first ascent of El Diente.

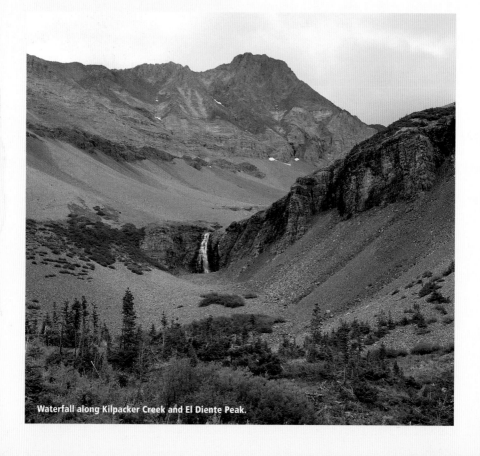

Waterfall along Kilpacker Creek and El Diente Peak.

El Diente from Dunton Road.

# Annotated Bibliography

American Alpine Club, *Accidents in North American Mountaineering 2009*, Golden, Colorado, 2009. This is an annual report edited by Jed Williamson that you should read every once in a while to remind yourself that you are mortal.

Borneman, Walter R. and Lampert, Lyndon J., *A Climbing Guide to Colorado's Fourteeners*, twentieth anniversary edition, Boulder, Colorado, Pruett Publishing Company, 1994. Now out of print, this was the most popular Fourteeners guidebook in the '70s and '80s.

Borneman, Walter R., and Caudle, Todd, *14,000 feet: A Celebration of Colorado's Highest Mountains*, Pueblo, Colorado, Skyline Press, 2005. The perfect coffee table book on the Fourteeners.

Clinger, Wade, *GPS Waypoints of Colorado's Fourteeners*, Boulder, Colorado, Pruett Publishing Company, 2000. Yup, all the waypoints you'd need to get yourself up a Fourteener in a whiteout ... if you are that nuts.

Colorado Fourteeners Initiative, *14ers.org*. An instructive web site by one of the major conservation organizations that works to rebuild trails on the Fourteeners.

Dawson, Louis W., *Dawson's Guide to Colorado's Fourteeners, Volume 1, The Northern Peaks*, Colorado Springs, Colorado, Blue Clover Press, 1994. Now out of print, but a must-have title if you want to climb and ski the Fourteeners in the winter.

Dawson, Louis W., *Dawson's Guide to Colorado's Fourteeners, Volume 2, The Southern Peaks*, Monument, Colorado, Blue Clover Press, 1996. See Dawson above.

Jacobs, Randy, and Ormes, Robert M., *Guide to the Colorado Mountains*, tenth edition, Golden, Colorado, Colorado Mountain Club Press, 2000. The legendary guidebook that belongs on every climber's bookshelf.

Middlebrook, Bill, *14ers.com*. The ultimate Fourteeners web site. A wonderful piece of work with a mind-boggling amount of detail on the routes, plus pictures.

Mountaineers, The, *Mountaineering: The Freedom of the Hills,* Seattle,Washington, Mountaineers Books, 2003. The mountaineering textbook. If you don't have one, buy one now.

Reed, Jack, and Ellis, Gene, *Rocks Above the Clouds: A Hiker's and Climber's Guide to Colorado Mountain Geology,* Golden, Colorado, Colorado Mountain Club Press, 2008. A detailed handbook on the geology of the Fourteeners, range by range.

Roach, Gerry, *Colorado's Fourteeners: From Hikes to Climbs,* second edition, Golden, Colorado, Fulcrum Publishing, 1999. The most detailed guidebook on the Fourteeners, with a variety of routes. One of the best guidebooks ever written.

Scott-Nash, Mark, *Colorado 14er Disasters: Victims of the Game,* Boulder, Colorado, Johnson Books, 2009. A veteran of Rocky Mountain Rescue Group tells stories of folks who ran out of luck on the Fourteeners.

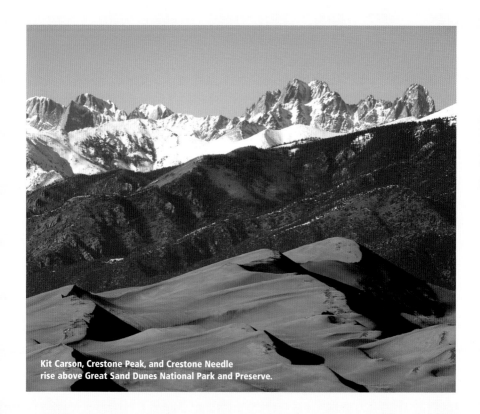

Kit Carson, Crestone Peak, and Crestone Needle
rise above Great Sand Dunes National Park and Preserve.

# Glossary

**AMS:** Acute Mountain Sickness—it happens to the best of us.

**BASIN:** a symmetrically dipping, elongated, circular flat area.

**CAIRN:** a pile of rocks, usually built by humans to mark a trail.

**CDT:** Continental Divide Trail.

**CFI:** The Colorado Fourteeners Initiative—the folks that help climbers and Fourteeners peacefully coexist.

**CMC:** The Colorado Mountain Club—your hosts for this guidebook.

**CMCF:** The Colorado Mountain Club Foundation.

**COL:** a small pass between two peaks.

**CONTOUR:** to traverse generally at a consistent elevation or slightly up or down.

**CORNICE:** an overhanging edge of snow on a ridge.

**COULOIR:** a steep gully or gorge frequently filled with snow or ice.

**EXPOSURE:** the empty space below a climber; the distance a climber would fall before doing a grounder.

**GLISSADE:** a usually voluntary act of sliding down a steep slope.

**GOATHEAD:** any climber who takes a dump and doesn't pack it out, or says, "Oh Buddy, we can make it," and pushes on in front of a thunderstorm.

**GULCH:** a deep V-shaped valley formed by erosion.

**HAPE:** High Altitude Pulmonary Edema—that gurgling sound.

**MORAINE:** sheets of rock debris transported by glaciers or ice sheets.

**PARIAH:** any self-absorbed amateur who cuts across switchbacks.

**POST-HOLING:** the art of repeatedly breaking through crusty snow, often up to the waist, while attempting to make forward progress.

**SADDLE:** a high pass between two peaks, larger than a col.

**SCREE:** loose, broken, unstable rock that climbers can never avoid.

**SLAB:** a relatively flat and featureless block of rock.

**TALUS:** (see scree)

**TUNDRA:** a treeless area where the dominant vegetation is grasses, mosses, and lichens.

**USFS:** US Forest Service.

**USGS:** United States Geological Survey.

# APPENDIX 1
# COLORADO FOURTEENERS RANKED BY HEIGHT

| MOUNTAIN | PAGE | ALTITUDE | RANGE |
|---|---|---|---|
| 1. Mount Elbert | 94 | 14,433 | Sawatch |
| 2. Mount Massive | 90 | 14,421 | Sawatch |
| 3. Mount Harvard | 114 | 14,420 | Sawatch |
| 4. Blanca Peak | 66 | 14,345 | Sangre de Cristo |
| 5. La Plata Peak | 98 | 14,336 | Sawatch |
| 6. Uncompahgre Peak | 162 | 14,309 | San Juan |
| 7. Crestone Peak | 50 | 14,294 | Sangre de Cristo |
| 8. Mount Lincoln | 78 | 14,286 | Mosquito |
| 9. Grays Peak | 26 | 14,270 | Front |
| 10. Mount Antero | 126 | 14,269 | Sawatch |
| 11. Torreys Peak | 26 | 14,267 | Front |
| 12. Castle Peak | 154 | 14,265 | Elk |
| 13. Quandary Peak | 74 | 14,265 | Mosquito |
| 14. Mount Evans | 30 | 14,264 | Front |
| 15. Longs Peak | 22 | 14,255 | Front |
| 16. Mount Wilson | 194 | 14,246 | San Juan |
| 17. Mount Shavano | 130 | 14,229 | Sawatch |
| 18. Mount Princeton | 122 | 14,197 | Sawatch |
| 19. Mount Belford | 102 | 14,197 | Sawatch |
| 20. Crestone Needle | 54 | 14,197 | Sangre de Cristo |
| 21. Mount Yale | 118 | 14,196 | Sawatch |
| 22. Mount Bross | 78 | 14,172 | Mosquito |
| 23. Kit Carson Peak | 42 | 14,165 | Sangre de Cristo |
| 24. El Diente Peak | 198 | 14,159 | San Juan |
| 25. (South) Maroon Peak | 146 | 14,156 | Elk |

| MOUNTAIN | PAGE | ALTITUDE | RANGE |
|---|---|---|---|
| 26. Tabeguache Peak | 130 | 14,155 | Sawatch |
| 27. Mount Oxford | 102 | 14,153 | Sawatch |
| 28. Mount Sneffels | 186 | 14,150 | San Juan |
| 29. Mount Democrat | 78 | 14,148 | Mosquito |
| 30. Capitol Peak | 134 | 14,130 | Elk |
| 31. Pikes Peak | 38 | 14,110 | Front |
| 32. Snowmass Mountain | 138 | 14,092 | Elk |
| 33. Mount Eolus | 182 | 14,083 | San Juan |
| 34. Windom Peak | 178 | 14,082 | San Juan |
| 35. Mount Columbia | 114 | 14,073 | Sawatch |
| 36. Missouri Mountain | 106 | 14,067 | Sawatch |
| 37. Humboldt Peak | 46 | 14,064 | Sangre de Cristo |
| 38. Mount Bierstadt | 34 | 14,060 | Front |
| 39. Sunlight Peak | 178 | 14,059 | San Juan |
| 40. Handies Peak | 174 | 14,048 | San Juan |
| 41. Culebra Peak | 70 | 14,047 | Sangre de Cristo |
| 42. Mount Lindsey | 58 | 14,042 | Sangre de Cristo |
| 43. Ellingwood Point | 66 | 14,042 | Sangre de Cristo |
| 44. Little Bear Peak | 62 | 14,037 | Sangre de Cristo |
| 45. Mount Sherman | 82 | 14,036 | Mosquito |
| 46. Redcloud Peak | 170 | 14,034 | San Juan |
| 47. Pyramid Peak | 150 | 14,018 | Elk |
| 48. Wilson Peak | 190 | 14,017 | San Juan |
| 49. Wetterhorn Peak | 166 | 14,015 | San Juan |
| 50. North Maroon Peak | 142 | 14,014 | Elk |
| 51. San Luis Peak | 158 | 14,014 | San Juan |
| 52. Mount of the Holy Cross | 86 | 14,005 | Sawatch |
| 53. Huron Peak | 110 | 14,003 | Sawatch |
| 54. Sunshine Peak | 170 | 14,001 | San Juan |

# APPENDIX 2
# COLORADO FOURTEENERS CLIMBING TICK LIST

| MOUNTAIN | PAGE | CLIMBING PARTNER | DATE |
|---|---|---|---|
| Longs Peak | 22 | | |
| Grays Peak | 26 | | |
| Torreys Peak | 26 | | |
| Mount Evans | 30 | | |
| Mount Bierstadt | 34 | | |
| Pikes Peak | 38 | | |
| Kit Carson Peak | 42 | | |
| Humboldt Peak | 46 | | |
| Crestone Peak | 50 | | |
| Crestone Needle | 54 | | |
| Mount Lindsey | 58 | | |
| Little Bear Peak | 62 | | |
| Blanca Peak | 66 | | |
| Ellingwood Point | 66 | | |
| Culebra Peak | 70 | | |
| Quandary Peak | 74 | | |
| Mount Lincoln | 78 | | |
| Mount Democrat | 78 | | |
| Mount Bross | 78 | | |
| Mount Sherman | 82 | | |
| Mount of the Holy Cross | 86 | | |
| Mount Massive | 90 | | |
| Mount Elbert | 94 | | |
| La Plata Peak | 98 | | |
| Mount Belford | 102 | | |

| MOUNTAIN | PAGE | CLIMBING PARTNER | DATE |
|---|---|---|---|
| Mount Oxford | 102 | | |
| Missouri Mountain | 106 | | |
| Huron Peak | 110 | | |
| Mount Harvard | 114 | | |
| Mount Columbia | 114 | | |
| Mount Yale | 118 | | |
| Mount Princeton | 122 | | |
| Mount Antero | 126 | | |
| Mount Shavano | 130 | | |
| Tabeguache Peak | 130 | | |
| Capitol Peak | 134 | | |
| Snowmass Mountain | 138 | | |
| North Maroon Peak | 142 | | |
| (South) Maroon Peak | 146 | | |
| Pyramid Peak | 150 | | |
| Castle Peak | 154 | | |
| San Luis Peak | 158 | | |
| Uncompahgre Peak | 162 | | |
| Wetterhorn Peak | 166 | | |
| Redcloud Peak | 170 | | |
| Sunshine Peak | 170 | | |
| Handies Peak | 174 | | |
| Windom Peak | 178 | | |
| Sunlight Peak | 178 | | |
| Mount Eolus | 182 | | |
| Mount Sneffels | 186 | | |
| Wilson Peak | 190 | | |
| Mount Wilson | 194 | | |
| El Diente Peak | 198 | | |